CONSOLATIONS

OF

SOLITUDE.

Os tenerum pueri balbumque poeta figurat;
Torquet ab obscenis jam nunc sermonibus aurem;
Mox etiam pectus præceptis format amicis;
Asperitatis et invidiæ corrector et iræ;
Rectè facta refert, orientia tempora notis
Instruit exemplis; inopem solatur et ægrum.
Q. Horatii Epist. prim. ad Augustum.

BOSTON:
JOHN P. JEWETT & COMPANY.
1856.

STEREOTYPED AT THE
BOSTON STEREOTYPE FOUNDRY.

DEDICATED

TO THE MEMORY OF

N. B. I.,

BY HIS SCHOOLMATE, CLASSMATE, AND FRIEND,

THE AUTHOR.

INTRODUCTION.

AUTHOR TO HIS BOOK IN EARLY SPRING.

Fly with the winds, frail leaves; the wintry hours
  Need ye no more; let green ones take your place,
Since Nature opes once more her book of flowers,
  And muffled February, with slow pace
Hobbling in storms away, lifts his white sock
  From the moist field; and now from all the hills
Trickles the new-thawed ice, and down the rock
  In every glen some crystal cataract spills;
The earth from its long sleep once more is free;
I, too, would break the spell of poesy.

Go, wanderers; I ask none to take ye in;
  But welcome all to harbor ye who will;
And whoso deems your value least to him,
  Is welcome most to leave ye fluttering still.

Farewell! on none intrude — the world is wide;
  Go uncommended, dressed in plain attire,
That none may save ye for a fair outside,
  Who, if mean clad, had cast ye to the fire.
If ye be worthless, ye shall die, no doubt;
If ye be worthy, worth shall find ye out.

TO THE READER.

If aught, here painted to thy soul or sight,
Of moral truth or natural scenes, delight,
Welcome! for thou art straight a comrade grown,
Who oft before hath walked with me unknown.
Yet if thy taste reject a thoughtful book,
Forbear upon these pictures e'en to look;
Seek not to know me, lest, thy labor o'er,
We grow more perfect strangers than before.

INDEX.

*** The brace connects the titles of certain poems placed side by side on account either of resemblance or contrast.

CONSOLATIONS OF SOLITUDE.

DEDICATION.

Tell me, thou cold and senseless clay,
 If speech can rend those realms of night,
Where Fate, that snatched thy breath away,
 Hides thee so darkly from my sight,

Where has the cheerful spirit fled
 Which made that mouldering form so dear?
Is it even like thine ashes dead?
 Lends it to love no listening ear?

Yet, since those moveless lips decline
 To answer from the earth's cold womb,
Speak, soul, thyself, and give some sign
 Shall pierce the mists that veil the tomb.

And whisper through the gloom profound,
 Say, dost thou value friendship yet?
Or, when thy temple fell to ground,
 Didst thou all love with life forget?

'Tis vain; no sound, no symbol speaks
 From those dull shades at mortal bid;
Well, then, till time the silence breaks,
 Still keep thy secret, wiselier hid.

If, purified from earthly stain,
 Thou hast no care for mortal lot, —
Lifted above all sense of pain,
 Sorrow and sin alike forgot, —

Then to the sacred past I'll fly,
 And to long-buried years go back,
In fancied youth will deem thee nigh,
 And meet thee in each wonted track.

If, mingled with the viewless wind,
 Both soul and sense have ceased to be,
Why, then, the faithful Muse must find
 Some moral prototype of thee.

And since were thine both truth and love,
  To truth and love shall she appeal;
Alas! though truth the sense approve,
  Love can no more be near to feel.

Howe'er, where'er, whate'er thou art,
  This tribute take — 'twas thine of old,
And to thine image in my heart
  I yield it now, since thou art cold.

And if the flame less bright will burn
  Than when by youthful impulse fired,
Fancy to friendship's torch could turn,
  And with new light become inspired, —

Still claim such gifts as Care permits,
  Since thou art fled, while day by day,
Fixed at my side she mutely sits,
  And twines the dark hair with the gray.

Speak, comrade — is there not, in truth,
  For faithful hearts some hallowed shore
Where, with the warmth of life's first youth,
  Old friends may yet shake hands once more?

None? then farewell; yet let my speech
  Seem not presumptuous nor profane;
Nor deem that selfishness can teach
  My heart to wish thee back again.

Yet, as the sailor's faithful hand
  Drags a few stones, with tears besprent,
And builds, upon some barren strand,
  To friendship a rude monument, —

So I, who mourned thy loss full long,
  Lone wandering where the sea of time
Sweeps drearier shores, now build in song
  This humble monument of rhyme.

ODE TO GOD,

AS HE APPEARS TO THE CHILD, AS HE RECEDES FROM THE YOUTH, AND AS HE RETURNS TO THE MAN.

Where shall I look for thee, since now no more
  I find thee at my side in human form?
Each day I'm floating farther from the shore
Of my fair land of dreams; life's summer's o'er,
          And thou art gone.

Ah, once from the blue waves how glowing bright
  Thy face uprose in yon fair orb of day!
And on the hill-top, with approaching night,
I saw thy parting smile in reddening light
          Melt slow away.

Fast by the holy font wouldst thou appear;
  Up the long aisle I saw thee as a dove;
In the grand organ I thy voice could hear;
Through painted windows saw thee shining clear;
          Thou wast all love.

And in dark night full oft — I scarce knew how —
  Thou cam'st in dreams, and, all unheard of men,
Named me thy child; thy bright wings fanned my brow;

Thou com'st at last no more — a Ruler now —
A Father then.

Wast thou not wont each year, on first of May,
To dress my flower plat, where the ice first thaws,
And drench my vines? Now, since thou'rt fled away,
Love does the work no more, but clouds of gray,
And natural laws.

Then I knew nought; the sky, the grove, the stream,
Were peopled all by phantasms; then I saw,
But sought no cause; things were but what they seem,
Yet few unlovely. Fancy's wayward dream
Explained each law.

No longer wilt thou smile nor stoop to bless,
But from afar each day dost set my task;
Each day thou growest greater, and I less;
Thou dost command, and if I acquiesce
Thou dost not ask.

Yet still I feel thee freshening in the breeze,
Still hear thee in each wave that sweeps the shore;
Still in thy works mine eye thy finger sees;

But now thou art the Master of all these—
Father no more.

Resounding on all sides thy praise I hear;
I see pale Terror kneel to kiss thy rod;
Yet sanctified far less by love than fear,
Man's worship dreads, but doth not deem thee dear,
Unlike that God

Whom love names "Father;" sages, "the All-wise;"
The afflicted, "Comforter;" while I've forgot
All titles for thee. With admiring eyes,
I see thine earth, thy seas, thy stars, thy skies,
And name thee not.

I feel thy wings upon the wintry blast;
I hear thy chariot in the rattling thunder—
Think on thine infinite worlds, so bright, so vast,
Thine endless future, and thy boundless past,
And mutely wonder.

Why should I dread thee, all-pervading mind?
Or whither go? Bereft of thee, how lone!
All dark without thy light, though with it blind,
I cannot fly thee, and I cannot find,
Thou wondrous one.

Forever round and round thy planets sail
  Thou'rt far away, yet ever near dost dwell;
Strange mystery! to solve thee I must fail;
I see thee, but can neither bid thee hail,
      Nor yet farewell.

But now methinks once more the mists profound
  Are scattering, and I see thy smile returning.
O, wonderful! mine eyes behold no bound;
Millions of stars encompass thee around,
      All brightly burning.

Each star a world, and all within thy sight
  In reverence mute from age to age revolving;
Spheres twinkling numberless, from night to night
Reflecting thine unfathomable light,
      Nor e'er dissolving.

All hail to thee once more! I see thy face
  Benignant still; but now thou dost appear
No longer shut within a narrow place,
But in each atom, through all boundless space,
      Again art near.

Parent once more! since, though beyond my sight,
  On unknown worlds thou shin'st, yet even there
A Parent still; they, too, in thee delight;

'Twas but thy brightness that begat my night;
Thou'rt every where.

Henceforth thus would I know thee, Sire of all,
Nor question make of thee; so speaks my heart.
All is in thee, and in thee nought can fall,
And thou in every thing, or great or small,
Wast, wilt be, art.

Yes, I again behold thee, night and day,
One and the same in wisdom as in will;
Watering my flowers once more in morning gray,
Melting at eve in mellow light away,
A Father still!

THE PHILOSOPHER IN SEARCH OF A RELIGION.

Forbear, O Faith, lest falsely thou direct
The unschooled reverence of a mind which sees
Thy votaries through the world, with blind respect
Bending the knee but to false deities,
And veneration made a senseless tool
In the misguiding hands of knave and fool.

If to the east I turn, the turbaned sage
  Meets me with sword in hand, and bids me place
My trust in selfish doctrines, and with rage
  Unbrotherly, wage war 'gainst half my race,
To gain a heaven, when from this earth I flee,
Whose bliss is beastly sensuality.

The Hindoo interrupts these brutish feasts,
  And calls me to his pest house at Banyan,
To spend my time in tending his sick beasts,
  And feeding vermin, dearer far than man,
That I may claim my dues of rats and mice,
When I am gone to his fool's paradise.

Another drives me from this patient task,
  To worship Mumbo Jumbo, or fall down
'Neath car of Juggernaut, or prostrate ask
  The favor of rude idols, and to crown
The head of bull, or ass, or grinning ape,
Whose hideousness transcends all beastly shape.

Another with remorseless hands would stain
  With human blood my altar, with raised knife,
Foul homage rendering; thus, like hated Cain,
  Death offering to the glorious source of life.
Another calls me to a different scene,
Where lewd Priapus holds his court obscene.

If from such scenes to Christian lands I look,
  To escape the bigot's zeal, 'tis still the same;
An hundred sects approach with cross and book,
  Each with a different doctrine, but one name.
Each bids me God in his own idol see,
Or in his demon seek my Deity.

If the dark page of history I explore,
  What horrid tale it tells! with what fierce speed,
Strife, Treachery, Hatred haste from shore to shore,
  Life in the doctrine, death in every deed!
Such mischiefs in each moment brought to birth,
The wonder is, man still should cumber earth.

Here, chained 'midst flaming fagots to the stake,
  The mangled martyr sinks in smothering fires;
There, locked in dungeons, for Christ's mercy's
    sake,
  'Midst shrieks and groans some tortured wretch
    expires,
Doomed with but this consoling thought to sink,—
That 'midst a senseless race he dared to think.

Here, Sorcery and Witchcraft spread their toils;
  There, Heresy would blast the good man's name;
While 'neath religion's cloak, grown fat on spoils,
  The priestly robber pilfers without shame,

And, with earth's potentates joined hand in hand,
Drives truth and virtue out from every land.

Here, cunning Avarice feigns to balance power,
  And steals from either side to make all even;
There, Craft monopolizes earthly dower,
  And pays the plundered with a pass to heaven,
And, on the spoils of others bloated grown,
Deeds lands in realms it ne'er shall see nor own.

How worthless an Elysium to the wise,
  Peopled by such! Sure 'twere small joy to meet
Tyrants and hypocrites, with upturned eyes,
  Puffing with pride on each celestial seat;
'Twere a far happier destiny to dwell,
With wise and good, in a more virtuous hell.

Lo, where, by all despised, the wandering Jew
  Views wistfully the lost land of his birth;
Faithful to old things rather than to new,
  Oppressed by all, he wanders o'er the earth;
Shunned e'en by him whose doctrine is but love;
Surely the serpent hath devoured the dove.

'Neath the red cross, Ham's sons, by Heaven's command,
  Water a stranger soil with sweat and tears;

Slaves 'neath the crescent, Japhet's children stand;
For truth in Spain grows falsehood in Algiers.
In each, to piety fraud makes profession;
Power never yet lacked reasons for oppression.

Still, Avarice in extortion must grow gray,
And Virtue fly to solitude from wrong;
For Innocence is Cunning's natural prey;
The weak find ever bloodhounds in the strong;
While Self, the hunter, with the whip of creed,
Halloo's his dogs to ravage at full speed.

See, through the world, what endless train of ills
Mankind to a blind fate ascribe; the wise,
To Ignorance, whom his own letter kills;
Doomed slave of craft, and with hoodwinkèd eyes,
Led on by armed Religion, to defend
Fraud, force, and hate, in guilt that hath no end.

Yet, when the book I open, and begin,
Through cloud of comment, the command to read,
" Let him who would cast stones be free from sin;"
" Clothe ye the naked, and the hungry feed;"
Or, " As ye love yourselves your neighbors love;"
Or, " Be ye perfect even as God above;"

Still farther when I read, "Do to another
As thou wouldst have another do to thee;"
And find that man is named of man the brother,
And all mere outcasts, who lack charity;
While God himself, proclaims from heaven above,
That his own government is based on love, —

Then do I learn that each man his own creed
Less from its doctrine than his heart derives;
'Tis still the wish is father to the deed;
Our gods are but the portraits of our lives;
And different natures, from the self-same law
Their different acts and different motives draw.

Yet, if from precepts, to great Nature's face
I turn my gaze, what glorious scene appears!
What beautiful diversity of race,
Through the wide world the boundless prospect cheers!
Herb, mineral, animal, in infinite kind,
Ranged orderly by one creative mind.

If I look farther, I perceive I stand
Upon a frail, unpropped, revolving ball,
Where sea is ever battling with the land,
Earth a mere crust, like an o'erarching wall
That spans a vault — so thin, almost a breath
The shell could shatter, flaming fire beneath.

And if I look beyond this narrow bound,
  Which seems to men so vast, through endless
      space,
I see, revolving ever round and round,
  Spheres following spheres, which whirl in endless
      race;
All, all afloat, yet all upheld, like me,
By the same law of central gravity.

And if, unwearied, still I strain my flight
  To soar beyond those milky drifts, where float
Worlds, numberless as snowflakes, filled with light,
  Each through blank space rowing its little boat,
Oarless and rudderless, yet each in time
Destined to reach its port by will divine, —

Great Father, have I found thee? There's no shore,
  Interminable space, yet light to light
Answering beyond for aye. I can no more;
  Fancy can find no wings for such a flight;
Thy beacon fires, more far than thought can flee,
Flash on and onward to infinity.

Now, to that spark would I look back once more,
  By men called Earth, pale glimmering as a star,
One moment bright, the next all clouded o'er,
  Scarce a mere speck, so infinitely far;

And now, my poor paternal acres, where,
Where are ye, that once cost me so much care?

Where what earth's fools name wealth? How passing small
Man's works! how weak his passions, vain his troubles!
Earth, sun, moon, stars, the heavens, mere nothings all;
The world itself, one of ten million bubbles,
Lit up by God's own beam, one moment bright;
'Tis all I know — the rest is dark as night.

Forbear! man's temples must be mine no more!
My fane I'll seek in yon blue vault immense;
Hymns in the chiming spheres; my search is o'er.
I've found him, but in such magnificence
That sight grows dark. His veil I cannot rend;
He lives, but without origin or end.

THE DYING VISION OF BENEDICT ARNOLD.

Come, pierce this bosom, welcome death!
  No enemy thou art;
Thou stiflest but the hated breath
  Of one, whose broken heart
No refuge finds but in despair;
Abhorred, detested, every where.

Where'er I go, men frown on me;
  I walk like Cain on earth;
All shudder when my face they see;
  Even in the halls of mirth,
At sight of me, the voices gay
In secret whispers die away.

When on some gala day I hear
  Men cry, "God save the king!"
The very mob, if I come near,
  Point at the hated thing,
Shrink at my vile name's very sound,
And empty space straight girds me round.

O that in hot pursuit close pressed,
I might but make my stand,
Bare to the stroke a warrior's breast,
And lift a warrior's hand,
And, bravely fighting with my foes,
Hail the swift shot that brought repose!

But no! I must not feel man's wrath;
My fate is more forlorn;
Each hastes in horror from my path,
Or stares in silent scorn;
And if a soldier meet my glance,
He turns his back as I advance.

If to my thoughts for peace I turn,
Still peace and I must part;
A hungry, never-dying worm
Is gnawing at my heart;
And conscience' self proclaims my ban,
Forever whispering, "Thou'rt the man."

When quiet night outspreads her wings,
I blush beneath the moon;
Refreshing morn no solace brings,
Nor the bright blaze of noon.
The very sun, as if in wrath,
Frowns like a shadow on my path.

Scarce do I deem, when I am dead
  I shall escape despair;
If in the grave I make my bed,
  Can there be peace even there,
For one, with whom the good, the just,
Deign not to mingle, even in dust?

Were there but hope to die unknown,
  That when the sexton's hand
Placed o'er my grave a nameless stone,
  I, in the stranger's land,
Might thus, even though by stealth, be sure
To moulder 'mongst the good and pure!—

But no! man's hate will grudge me stones
  My fate hath long been sealed;
Scarce will the ploughman let my bones
  Lie scattered on his field,
Lest they should breed his harvest's bane,
Wither his grass, and blight his grain.

Poor André, whom untimely fate
  Cut off in manhood's prime!
In brooding on my lonely state,
  How do I envy thine!
For thou wast loved and mourned, at least,
Not shunned like some wild, treacherous beast.

O, native land, forever lost!
For thee I heave no sigh,
Yet still must think at what dear cost
I'm forced from thee to fly;
Doomed to a traitor's deathless fame,
Millions unborn shall curse my name.

My sword is rusty with the gore
Of countrymen and brothers;
I've made full many a sire deplore
And many weeping mothers;
But this I long have ceased to prize;
In my revenge none sympathize.

Curst day, when to our foes I fled!
Scarce had I left the boat,
When each that knew me turned more red
Than his own scarlet coat.
The men drawn up before my tent,
Blushed at the order, "Arms present."

And when, the foremost in the fight,
I bade all bravely stand,
Each officer looked black as night;
All shrunk from my command,
And would have served, I well could see,
Under a dog more soon than me.

The ungrateful knaves for whom I bled,
  Scowled at me when I passed;
They grudged that swords my blood should shed,
  Still longing to the last
To see me by the halter strung,
And to the hounds, like carrion, flung.

I hate them all; I hate mankind;
  Hate every living thing;
Yet, though to infamy consigned,
  Still to my pride I cling.
O soul! be stubborn, nor deplore
The loss of honor, thine no more.

The thirst of gold hath been my bane;
  Yet not that wealth I prize,
But rank and power I sought to gain;
  All these I now despise.
There's not a man so poor, so mean,
That would as Arnold's guest be seen.

No! should I meet the very groom
  Did once my stables tend,
He, too, would give me elbow room,
  But scorn to be my friend.
Would that in earth I might but rot,
Alike by God and man forgot.

My life is like a darksome night,
   A cave without a vent;
No glimmering streak of cheerful light
   Across my track is sent,
To dash the gloom through which I stray
With a few drops of transient day.

I will not shed unmanly tears;
   Yet, like the wandering Jew,
Might I but roam ten thousand years,
   And then my life renew,
A happy, careless child once more —
But no; the days of hope are o'er.

Peace, soldier, peace! these transports cool;
   Let men deride thy name;
Thou conquered'st armies; wherefore, fool,
   Canst thou not conquer shame?
Fall at thy post, nor feel regret;
Be thy soul's heaven but to forget.

And though thine enemies thy head
   To carrion crows may give,
They do to thee but that, when dead,
   They dared not when alive.
So the mind sleep, let crows refresh
Their hungry stomachs with my flesh.

My senses reel; a flickering mist
  Like dusk o'erspreads mine eyes;
But hark! what steps approach? Hist, hist!
  Armed files around me rise.
Comrades, forgive, and grasp my hand;
What, none! all mute and shuddering stand!

Then, since none other deigns me touch,
  Despatch me, Death, at last;
Once I'd have done for thee as much;
  Thy firelock load — stand fast!
Now give me all my soul's desire;
Captain, make ready, aim, and fire!

THE LAST MOMENTS OF NATHAN HALE.[1]

One short half hour — 'tis all is left
  Of my brief soldier life;
Then must I fall, of sense bereft,
  While o'er my grave the strife
Shall rage as fiercely as before,
But me the trump shall wake no more.

No friend will follow in the host
That bears me forth to death;
'Midst jeering foes I yield my ghost;
Rough hands will choke my breath.
There's none 'mongst all that see me die
Will drop a tear or heave a sigh.

Yet were I firm save but for one,
Who loves me, far away.
O mother! thou wilt mourn thy son,
Lamenting night and day;
Yet thou shalt learn, with sorrowing pride,
Thy soldier triumphed as he died.

'Tis true, the gallows' highway seems
An ill road to the grave;
'Tis true, my manhood's morning dreams
A fairer promise gave,
And bade me leap at freedom's call —
In her first ranks to fight and fall.

Yet to the wise it matters nought
What way he goes to dust;
The sole thing worthy of his thought
Is, if his cause be just;
And if he's right, he'll act, nor think
Whether he's doomed to swim or sink.

Dear country, nought in death I dread,
  Save that but once I fall,
And slumber idly with the dead,
  When thou hast need of all;
Thy living sons shall all defend,
While I with senseless earth must blend.

Thy cause requires a million hands
  To battle with thy foes,
Lives numerous as the ocean sands;
  I have but one to lose.
Yet, though the sacrifice be small,
Disdain not, since I give thee all.

O that my blood from out the ground,
  'Neath God's inspiring breath;
Might at thy trumpet's piercing sound
  One instant leap from death,
Each drop a man, each man a spy,
Foredoomed in thy great cause to die

How blest even so to serve thee still,
  Slain o'er, and o'er, and o'er!
From field to field, from hill to hill,
  I'd chase thy cannon's roar,
And shed my blood like showers of rain,
And fall, and rise, and fall again.

And when from all thy foes once more
  Thy blood-stained soil was free,
And hill and dale, from shore to shore,
  In peace dwelt tranquilly,
Gladly I'd die with war's last thunder,
And soundly sleep thy green earth under

But hark! I hear the muffled drum
  Roll like a smothered wave;
And there the columns marching come
  That bear me to my grave.
Farewell, dear native land! this heart
Feels but one pang as now we part.

I only grieve because my eyes
  Thy glory may not see —
That I can serve thee but with sighs,
  Nor more lift sword for thee;
And mourn because life's fleeting breath
Permits me but a single death.

Farewell, dear friends! sweet light, farewell!
  Earth, take once more thy child;
Brief is the tale my life can tell;
  Thou hast me undefiled.
Death, I forgive thine early spoil;
Thanks that I sleep on mine own soil.

Sergeant, I come; and now once more,
  And once again, farewell!
Land of my birth, I love thee more,
  O, more than tongue can tell!
Now love's last dying gift receive;
Alas! I've nought but love to leave.

RETROSPECT.

THE gulf's far shore my straining sight
  Scarce reaches, through the deepening shades,
And mingling with the growing night,
  The gorgeous glow of evening fades.
The lowing kine have ceased their moan;
  The furnace fires have lit the brine;
And the quick chimes, with cheerful tone,
  Ring the ninth hour of evening time.

The marshy tribes renew their tune,
  And spring with fragrance fills the breeze;
And in full sail the ascending moon
  Glides on her course through airy seas.
And now the sister Pleiads sink;
  The lighthouse beacons flash and fade;

And bending o'er the water's brink,
  The cedars frown in darker shade.

And once again through streaming tears
  My thoughts retrace their ancient track,
And through the mists of by-gone years
  To well-remembered scenes go back.
This is the spot — I marked it well;
  Thy face was sad, thine eyes were wet,
When, thy voice mingling with the bell,
  Breathed its "Good bye," and "Don't forget."

Dim on the wave thy barge receded,
  And bore thee swiftly from the shore,
And the light breeze brought back unheeded
  The sullen plashing of the oar;
But when once more I stood alone,
  Where both so oft of old had met,
Silence recalled thy look and tone;
  "Fear not," I said; "I'll not forget."

Long years have swept our lives between;
  I've looked for thee, and found thee not;
Lost thee in many a waking dream,
  Till I half wished thou wert forgot.
Oft while the bird of night sings clear,
  And the pale mists sweep o'er the wave,

Thy voice comes sighing on mine ear,
  Like a sad whisper from the grave.

How oft I've stood and scanned the bay,
  And fancied thou wert ferrying o'er —
Seen the tides swell and sink away;
  And when I knew thou wast no more,
Still faithful to unfriendly time,
  I'd haunt the beach that skirts the main,
And hear the hope-deceiving chime
  Sing, "He will yet come back again."

"Forget me not!" Ah, not alone
  The yearning heart or plaintive bells
Echo those words; with solemn tone
  All nature's voice the chorus swells,
Thy mournful warning fain to mock
  With myriad tongues of subtle skill,
Which, restless as the ticking clock,
  Keep the tired mind remembering still.

The fading flower, the withering leaf,
  Yon mouldering arch, those grassy graves,
Comrades resigned with tears and grief,
  Some laid in earth, some whelmed in waves,
Old friends, whom now estranged I see,
  The time-worn clock that tells the hour,

Those trunks of many a mouldering tree,
The roofless cot, the ruined tower; —

The murmuring wave, the autumn breeze,
Those wedged ranks which high o'erhead
In screaming armies cross the seas,
Each tolling bell that wails the dead;
Old faces, once so fresh and bright,
Now sallow, wrinkled, lean, and wan,
Each parting day, each passing night,
All works of nature or of man; —

Sorrows and cares, that will not slumber,
Sweet life, that like yon sun must set,
And faults and follies without number,
All ceaseless clamoring, "Don't forget!
Ah, friend, if wearied memory clings,
With its first fondness thus to thee,
'Midst hosts of so distracting things,
That memory must immortal be!

Yet, as the primrose scents the air
More sweetly when the sun is fled,
Remembrance thus to my despair
Makes thee more dear that thou art dead.
Thine image flits amongst these trees;
Yon chimes each evening ring thy knell;

And o'er the dusky bay, the breeze
  Comes laden with thy last farewell.

Hark! The deep bells once more are pealing;
  The winds are hushed, the waves are bright;
And, o'er the dreamy waters stealing,
  That voice, upon the wings of night,
Names me once more. Old friend, I'm near;
  Speak once again; O, fly not yet!
'Tis hushed; no other sound I hear,
  Save that faint whisper, "Don't forget."

But now no lingering beam betrays
  The footsteps of the sunken sun;
And, through the soft and silvery haze,
  The stars come twinkling one by one.
Farewell! yet if I might behold,
  Through the long past without regret,
All fair as thou — but eve grows old;
  I must remember to forget.

THE LAMENT OF ORPHEUS.

WHAT now avails it me,
To have been born of thee,
Calliope? O, why so well
Learned I to touch the tuneful shell,
By thee, and by thy sister muses taught?
Ah, woful day, when first these fingers caught
From great Apollo's hand the lyre so richly wrought!

And what avails it now
To have smoothed the rugged brow
Of the fierce dragon, that in sleep
Forgot what he was set to keep,
While 'neath the cliffs, above our heads that hung,
The hard-bound ship upon the waves I swung,
And the rocks ceased to move, and listened while I sung?

Or that in Thracian cave,
Immured in living grave,
I tamed the rude, ferocious race,
That roamed like beasts about the place,
Softening their rage to sympathetic mood,
Till to unwonted tears they were subdued,
Leaving their bloody rites for mutual brotherhood.

Ye gods! why thus unjust
To them that in ye trust?
Did not I first from tinklings vain
Turn Music's voice to heavenly strain,
And teach the sacred hymn on earth to sound?
Sorrow is all the recompense I've found,
Ever the fate of those whose brows with bays are crowned.

Not soon shall I forget
The horrors of that pit;
The demons, round me gathering fast,
Winked at each other when I passed,
And, sneering, said, "Here comes one more to dwell
With the delightful brotherhood of hell!"
But all the din grew hushed when thee I woke, sweet shell!

Now must I mourn for thee,
Poor lost Eurydice!
Serpent shall never sting thee more,
Roving that dark and joyless shore.
Ah, how each listening ghost, 'midst twilight pale,
Wailed, gazing from his melancholy jail!
While Charon, resting on his oar, forgot to sail.

The torturers, at the tone,
Seemed as if changed to stone,
And backward turned to hear the strain,
And dropped their instruments of pain.
Those sooty depths ne'er heard such sounds before;
The very damned dared dream of bliss once more,
And, in amazement hushed, some time forgot to roar.

The blood-born sisters listening,
Their eyes with pity glistening,
Looked upward from their iron bench,
And ceased the mangled wretch to wrench;
Their dark cheeks were bestained with crimson tears;
The clustering snakes uncoil; each, as he hears,
Hangs flouting to the time, prone o'er his mistress' ears;

Until all, soothed to rest,
Droop down each Fury's breast;
While through the vast unechoing deep,
Pain and despair were hushed to sleep;
And the charmed dog, on his three chins asprawl,
Crouched to the ground, and toward the sounds 'gan crawl,
Low whining to the chords, in many a lengthening drawl.

Sweet lyre, thou even didst move
The pitying Fates above,
Till Atropos attentive hears,
Looks up, and on inverted shears
Rests her lean hand, and with a long-drawn sigh,
Says, " Let the poor thing go ; she shall not die ;
Go both, be free, but look not backward while ye fly."

I heard those words of peace,
Solace, ere long, to cease ;
Full soon, alas ! upon my tongue
The glad Eureka died unsung.
Yet now, ere from these glooms we 'gan to creep,
What fearful silence filled the murky deep,
Those wastes so still that even the Furies fell asleep!

But while, in silent pleasure,
I clasped my long-lost treasure,
Those dreadful women woke, full fain
To be at their old task again ;
The tear, half started, in their eyes shrunk back ;
The writhing snakes grew to a deeper black,
And, at full length outstretched, loud hissed along our track.

Again the mournful cries
All round about us rise;
Loud Charon chides his lingering train;
Awakened pity sleeps again;
And, as we hasten through the gates of hell,
Far off the red-eyed dog begins to yell,
And with his bark, sweet bride, is blent thy last farewell.

Swift as a flash of light,
Snatched to the realms of night,
With anguished looks and outstretched hands,
She mingles 'mongst the infernal bands;
And, on their screaming hinges turning round,
Loud crashed the ponderous gates, with awful sound;
And echo with ten thousand thunders, shook the ground.

O, why remember more,
Since time will ne'er restore
Life's lost delights? Let men from this
Learn not to trifle with their bliss.
I deemed her mine; my toil was almost crowned
Forgetful but one instant, I looked round,
And lost my all for aye, even at woe's farthest bound.

Learn from my doom to obey;
In fortune's brightest day,
Let no one count on certain joy;
Fate in an instant can destroy;
And though with tuneful art thy master skill
All hell entrance, and make the heavens grow still,
All shall be nought to him who once forgets Jove's will.

TO THE SHADE OF SAMUEL ADAMS.[2]

PATRIOT and sage! forgive ungrateful time,
Whose wing so darkly o'er thy memory broods;
Nor be thy ghost disturbed because this rhyme
Upon thy sacred privacy intrudes,
From mists of years thus dragging forth the name
Of one who from the insulting breath of Fame
Had shrunk, as if good deeds, when trumpeted, were shame.

Yet would I men might more revere that band,
Whose heroes, self forgetting, seek for good
But in great principles, since Nature's hand
Forms such so sparingly, least understood,
Rarest of all her works in human form.

How few are in whole generations born,
Who can like heroes live, while yet the name they
scorn!

Which one of all thine acts shall I first mention?
Which of thy sayings first? since to relate
Great things of thee doth not demand invention.
Self didst thou sacrifice to save the state;
Yet this men know; and now I would recall
Forgotten things, if so it may befall,
By lesser stars eclipsed, thou shalt not perish all.

But scarcely for thy sake, since thou wert last
'Mongst men to wish in mouths of men to be.
Yet would I that the virtue of the past
Live to inspire a late posterity,
Till, grown in love with justice, men may deem
Still best to be whate'er 'tis best to seem,
Lest truth be deemed a name, and virtue but a
dream.

Shall I relate how, while e'en yet a youth,
The rights of man by thee were understood,
Arguing that much-vexed question, if, forsooth,
Men may resist the laws?[3] "If public good
Demand it, then they may, and, to be free,
O'erthrow the rulers." Thus, though young, by thee
Foreshadowed was the march of human liberty.

Or shall I tell how trifling in thine eyes
 Seemed worldly wealth?[4] Yet, that thou didst not fall
A slave to mammon will no man surprise,
 In one who for the nation's good gave all,
Preferring to live poor, so it might be,
When he was gone, his country might live free;
The wise will surely smile should I tell this of thee.

Or that with bribes they tempted thee in vain
 The sacred cause of freedom to betray?[5]
In vain with threats would bend thee; that the stain
 Of traitor lay not on thee, shall I say?
This were to class thee with that bankrupt tribe
Whom men reward when debts are satisfied;
O, no! to praise thee thus were only to deride.

For how shall rank or riches him seduce,
 Whom his own safety tempts not? Yet I joy
In those proud words thou spakest, when abuse
 They heaped on thee, even threatening to destroy.
When in thine ear, "Expect no pardon," rings,
Thou say'st, "Think not that I shall fear such things;

My peace has long been made with the great King
of kings." [6]

Was not thy soul delighted on that day,
When the alarm bells rang from every steeple,
And thou to the scared governor didst say,
"I wait thine answer to the impatient people?" [7]
While he, abashed, quailed thy stern glance
beneath,
And men scarce dared break silence by a breath,
Thou, fixed as fate, resolved on liberty or death.

No less 'tis true that, throughout all the land,
Thou soughtest in one will all men to bind,[8]
That each by each in brotherhood might stand,
And that the struggle o'er, thou wast resigned
To live obscure; men needed thee no more.
So live the unselfish when, all danger o'er,
The world, grown safe, goes back to vanity once
more.

Nor less devoted wast thou on that day
When, through the plains of Lexington, thy
foes,
In many a troop, did circumvent thy way.
Bright o'er the hills the beauteous sun uprose;
Freedom's first gun was fired, and thou didst say

To thy companion, "'Tis a glorious day!"[9]
He answered, "Yes, 'tis beautiful," but thou saidst,
"Nay,

"I meant not that, though every work of God,
'Tis true, is beautiful; but for this land,
I meant, a glorious day. Henceforth the rod
Of tyranny is broke, and we shall stand,
As God means man shall stand, self-ruling, free;
Henceforth our country shall a refuge be
For all the oppressed on earth whose hearts love
liberty."

Perchance the hope of freedom for mankind
Is but a dream, and nations doomed to be
Forever led in blindness by the blind;
If so, still all the more I honor thee,
And men like thee, who, though they cannot know
Whether our race shall to perfection grow,
Ne'er lose their trust in good, but hope it shall
be so.

Prosperity ne'er found thee too elate;
Adversity still met thee undepressed;
Pure was thy life above all fear of fate;
Thy heart was true, thy soul so self-possessed,
That if the earth but one man owned like thee,

And all beside should slaves and tyrants be,
He had loved virtue still; such through all time
are free.

Didst thou not say, " If, of a thousand, all[10]
Must sink in freedom's struggle, save but one,
Best still to fight, best the whole race should fall,
Save one free household; liberty alone,
Grafted on such a stock, would give creation
To happiness more great than a whole nation
Of cowering slaves could feel through a long generation."

Such was thy thought. Freedom thou hadst defended,
Till to the polar seas thou hadst been pressed;
And when her reign upon the land was ended,
Thou wouldst have climbed the glassy iceberg's
breast,
And, on thy crystal raft, hadst sought repose
In frozen regions, where no herbage grows,
And the white bear roams wild, midst everlasting
snows.

Such once men knew thee, though thy name, o'ergrown
With weeds of time, hath rusted in this age;

Yet would I speak of some few things less known,
Nor e'er yet written upon history's page;
Alas, how few! because thou gav'st to flame [11]
Each record, howe'er precious to thy fame,
Which on another's cheek could raise the blush of shame.

Yet some wise words, by filial reverence 'shrined
In memory's casket, would the muse unfold,
Though trifling. Sure thy shade no fault will find,
But rather smile that such things should be told,
Unless with Hampden and with Sidney met,
Rejoicing 'neath a sun that doth not set,
Thou, at great freedom's fount, all things of earth forget.

I would relate thy words upon that day,
When some were mourning for that fragrant weed,
Which now in Neptune's cauldron boiling lay.
They deemed it hard to flout the people's need,
And waste their wealth on ocean's deity,
Who scarce would thank them, while he quaffed their tea.
Why full-fed comfort yield for a starved liberty?

Then 'mongst the citizens didst thou arise,
And say, "To selfish counsels give no heed;
Lust not for Egypt's flesh pots, but be wise;
Be free alike in thought, and word, and deed.
Let us abandon bread if needs must be,
And like our ancestors, by yon blue sea,
Feast on her cast up clams, ere we pay tax on tea." [12]

Wise also were the words which thou one day
Didst to thy daughter utter. "Father," said she,
"Answer this question: Do they rightly say,
Who bid us shun all singularity?"
"In trifles to be strange," thou saidst, "were rude,"
Then smiling, thou didst add, "be't understood [13]
'Tis right, my child, that we be singularly good."

Such was thy thought, when men once strove to unloose [14]
Thy horses, and, through reverence, in their place
Harnessed themselves; amazed, thou didst refuse
Farther to go, and at the deep disgrace
Indignant blushing, didst exclaim, "Give o'er!
If we are beasts, not men, let us restore

To our lost lords their mules, and bondage claim
once more."

Not spoken vauntingly, thou wast impelled
By love of thine own kind; the rights of men
By thee were in such estimation held,
That life, without them, but as death had
been.
Still, lenient in all trifling things, from thee
Well-meaning weakness needed ne'er to flee;
Guilt only feared thy frown, and soulless tyranny.[15]

Yet why should I such things of thee relate?
They scarce can add new lustre to thy name;
I would not that a life so truly great
Seem blown to greatness by the breath of Fame,
Which cannot more ennoble men like thee;
Such scarce are honored by celebrity.
O, no! true virtue still its own reward must be.

I'm glad thou didst die poor, that flattery's voice
Deigns scarcely to applaud; for if the upright
Might always in prosperity rejoice,
Life would no moral point, would shed no light;
Selfish and wise would be as one, and then
The good would seem but what the bad have
been —

Well doers, not for good's sake, but to be seen of
men.

Here will I leave thee, then, without a sigh
For what is lost, but what lives of thee cherish;
Since with thy words thine influence shall not die,
I am content; thou shalt not wholly perish;
Each good life doth lost faith in good restore,
And that good men have lived, though now no
more,
Impels to greater worth than earth hath known
before.

Sleep on! no monument of marble pride
To mark thy grave, no flattering tongues nor
pens
To praise thee; thus thou wouldst have lived —
thus died —
One amongst undistinguished citizens.
Thy memory sacred in their hearts shall be,
Who through all time most reverence liberty;
And who best love mankind will ever best love
thee.

No idle statue apes thine air — no bust [16]
Mocks thy calm smile. Thou died'st with good
outworn,

And o'er the uncolumned tomb that holds thy
dust [17]
Thousands of freemen pass each night and morn,
Trampling the pavement with unceasing tread
In never-ending armies o'er thy head,
To whom thy very name is, like thine ashes, dead.

What matters it? Thy wishes are fulfilled.
A living tide sweeps o'er thee like a wave;
And Freedom, for whom so much blood was
spilled,
Seems chanting thus the requiem o'er thy grave:
"These streams of life were first inspired by thee;
Thou taughtest first the fathers to be free.
Be this thy monument — the children's liberty."

THE NUPTIALS:

OR, MARRIAGE OF THE TRUE AND BEAUTIFUL.

I saw, as in a waking dream,
When mingles morn with night,
The sun and moon, with mutual beam,
Burst on my dazzled sight;
And wide unrolling in the blaze,
The heavens seemed open to my gaze.

And a fair maid, of graceful mien,
 Stood with a youth in white;
And all around heaven's hosts were seen,
 Clothed in celestial light.
The skies with sphery music rang,
And all the stars together sang.

But soon the strains more softly flow,
 And in rich cadence close,
When Heaven's high priest, in robes of snow,
 Upon his feet uprose;
The hosts closed round him like a cloud,
While thus he raised his voice aloud:—

"Wilt thou, O Truth, this maiden take
 To be thy wedded wife,
And, all renouncing for her sake,
 Make glad with her thy life?"
He spoke, and all the heavens grew still.
Truth answered, cheerfully, "I will."

"Beauty, wilt thou," the archangel cried,
 "Accept this willing youth?
Wilt thou renounce all loves beside,
 And cling for aye to Truth,
Content his days to adorn and bless?"
And Beauty, blushing, answered, "Yes."

Then, with a shout that shook the skies,
  Rejoiced the seraph bands ;
The two stood mute, with downcast eyes ;
  The archangel joined their hands,
And blessed them both, and said, " 'Tis done;
Beauty and Truth, henceforth be one."

As for what more I saw, if aught,
  My senses have forgot ;
And oft I ponder in my thought,
  If 'twere a dream or not.
Yet when the Beautiful I view,
She still seems wedded to the True.

TO A SNOW-COVERED APPLE TREE.

Poor trunk, half hid in snowy wreath,
  So late my favorite tree,
When your red-fruited boughs beneath
  I rested carelessly —

How mournfully the howling blast,
  This desolated scene,
And that cold, icy cowl, contrast
  With days when you were green !

Here plucked I the first flowers of spring,
  Here took my summer's nap;
Whilst you in playfulness would fling
  Your apples in my lap;

Or with a sudden whisper break
  The sleep that bound too long,
When cuckoos through the groves would wake
  Their rain-foretelling song.

And here, through autumn's golden hours,
  You've cast your ripened store,
And ere half gathered, with new showers,
  Would still give more and more.

And oft, to make dull days rejoice,
  With tales the time you'd cheer;
And still more lively grew your voice
  As winter grew more near.

And when October, clear and cold,
  Had chilled my grassy seat,
How oft you've plucked your locks of gold,
  And cast them at my feet!

Whene'er with friends, in pleasant speech,
  I 'neath your shade reclined,

Your outstretched arms o'er all would reach,
  In benediction kind.

And if the fate of loved ones dead,
  At eve we would recall,
In dews, upon each downcast head,
  How fast your tears would fall!

And while we've talked of days gone by,
  Or spoke in freedom's cause,
How oft you've answered with a sigh,
  Or murmured your applause!

Here was I wont to quaff my wine,
  So luscious to the taste—
A present from the graceful vine
  That clung around your waist,—

And still who clings, and seems to love,
  Though faded all your charms,
Still reaching these deep snows above,
  To clasp you in her arms.

Yet why should I bewail you here,
  Or mourn o'er your decay,
Since the fond friends that made you dear
  Have also passed away?

An equal fate we're doomed to know;
  The self-same lot we share;
You stand forlorn in wastes of snow,
  And I in wastes of care.

Time's frosts must bleach my locks of black,
  As snows have blanched your bough;
To vanished joys we both look back,
  And ask, "Where are they now?"

THE ASSABET BROOK AND RIVER.[18]

Born on hills, and nursed by springs,
Its little waves, like outstretched wings
Feathered with foam, all snowy white,
Waft it adown, how swift! how light!
From uplands brown, where browsing flocks
Crop a scant meal amongst the rocks,
To meadows green, and fertile fields,
Where earth her richest harvest yields,
Until its waters, clear and cool,
Enter my favorite bathing pool,
Where in such still content they lie,
Reflecting a scarce ruffled sky,

That in calm days the place might pass
For fair Narcissus' looking-glass.
All mute, save where a tinkling fall
Spills amongst hemlocks dark and tall,
And round the roots of each old tree
Curls with a whispering melody.
Or where the trunk of blasted pine,
Wreathed around with many a vine,
All of boughs and bark bereft,
Weak and trembling, spans the cleft;
While yet another mounted higher,
Propped by green banks of sweetbrier,
Quakes beneath the trembling hands
Of him that on the frail bridge stands;
And there, the tottering rail below,
The limpid waters wreathing flow;
Now hid from sight in piny shroud,
Now 'neath the light and quivering cloud
Of bending aspens glimmering pale,
Where swift the fleecy foam balls sail,
Till, with the current clear and thin,
They plunge my little basin in,
And on the pool so smooth and deep
Lie settled in a tranquil sleep.

That pool, so pleasant to the sight,
At last shall stranger eyes delight,

Since now the artist's skilful hand[19]
Hath made its placid breast expand
In mimic floods, on painted vales,
Where winds the rill through sepia dales;
And now its little cataracts rush
O'er barriers built with pen and brush.
'Midst penciled woods and inky grass,
Unheard, though seen, its waters pass,
And oft recall, in wintry hours,
Its merry route 'twixt banks of flowers.

But endless peace on earth below
Were bliss nor thou nor I must know;
Fate such boon hath granted not
Or to man's or nature's lot.
Thou, too, bright and beauteous stream,
Oft dost lose thy look serene,
Destined in a sterner course,
Force to overcome with force.
When, beneath a three days' shower,
Driven before the freshet's power,
Who shall dare thy waves restrain,
Lashed along by wind and rain?
Then the whirlpool, boiling round,
Swells above the basin's bound;
Bursting through its prison doors,
Down the rocky gulf it roars,

And the waves so wildly toss,
Human footsteps dare not cross.

Thus, in spring time's earliest green
Assabet's fair brook is seen,
Ere its greater namesake hides
In her breast its tiny tides;
But when both their floods combined,
In a river's strength are joined,
Then its voice more silent grows;
In a deeper bed it flows,
Sweeping on through glen and glade,
Now in light, and now in shade,
Plunging here 'neath buzzing mill,
There in broad pool resting still;
Till at last, in Acton's vale,
Scarce the current seems to sail,
And its azure breast expands
To a placid lake, and stands
So still, that scarce a tiny wave
Ripples above the river's grave.
There from the east, with solemn frown,
Sudbury's pine-clad hills look down;
While to the west, in shadows deep,
The fields long after sunrise sleep.

Sweet, in the morn of sultry day,
To that o'erarching shade to stray,

Where the causeway shoots across,
Flanked with elms in all its course;
While circling slow round islands green,
Fixed their foamy tracks between,
Poured through channels three, the torrent
Rushes in a triple current;
One checked at night, when, shut across,
The sluicegate bars the water's course;
One almost dead, save when it drains
The vernal snows and autumn rains;
While through the third the full stream gushes,
And to its steep plunge boldly rushes;
And as the torrent wildly tears
Down its rocky flight of stairs,
Low on either margin bending,
Drooping elms, their dark boughs blending,
Lock their long arms the gorge across,
And as the breeze-fanned branches toss,
The green leaves fluttering to and fro,
But half conceal the surge below,
Whiter than the drifted snow;
While the pale mists, all silvery gray,
Brood o'er the gulf of boiling spray.

Sweeter, on some still night in June,
When full grown leaves half hide the moon,
And all the house is wrapped in sleep,
From my chamber window seat

To view without the cheerful night,
And see the ripples glancing bright,
When the dripping wheel hangs still
In the crazy old gristmill,
Where, trickling 'mongst the mouldering beams,
The flood sinks in an hundred streams;
While to the tune the screech owl shrill
Cries from the orchard 'neath the hill,
And the near cataract all night long
Lulls the ear with murmuring song.

Most beauteous, when the uprisen sun
Tarries awhile the hills among;
First, through the woods his struggling beam
Glances the gloomy pines between,
Where, towering up the steep ascent,
Their tall tops sweep the firmament.
But soon the rays spill softly o'er,
And stream along the opposing shore,
Scattering in air the misty wreath
That broods upon the lake beneath,
On whose fair bosom night and day
Both at once their charms display,
Gleaming half like molten gold,
Shrouded half in shadows cold;
While the broad hill, so darkly brown,
Dips in the wave its pine-capped crown,
And dives full many a fathom down.

Such, at least in days of yore,
Was the look the landscape wore;
Such a look it wears no more.
Long ago the hand of man
Lopped the elm trees from the dam,
Swept the forest from the hill,
Closed the sluiceway, shut the mill;
All its beauties are defaced;
Now the scene's a naked waste.
Sweet Acton vales and woods, farewell!
No more the autumn breeze shall swell
Through your green boughs; I see no sign
Of all I loved in olden time,
Save where e'en yet the maples sigh
To the swift river sweeping by,
Or where the flume, with its dull moan,
Lends to the winds a deeper tone.
No more, through boughs the walks that lined,
I see the millwheel far behind,
In its white halo whirling round,
While the swift clapper's lively sound
Blent with the roar of the bright fall
That glittered through its leafy wall.

Still on the river's banks below,
Where, near the verge, the ball flowers blow,[20]
The little gravel walk that winds
Close on the brink, e'en yet reminds

Of those loved days when, all alone,
I, as a school boy, far from home,
Through the green path each morn would roam,
While o'er the wave the grapevines hung,
Far out of reach; how tempting swung
The purple clusters, fain to sweep
The frothy flakes from out the deep,
So low they dangled; till at last,
An hundred lovely arbors past,
The flowery footpath devious wound
To a lone meadow, where no sound
Broke on the ear; where, broad and high,
Dense-wooded hills cut off the sky;
And here the stream flowed mute as death;
The very storm winds held their breath,
And human feet drew seldom near;
The autumn breeze scarce whispered here;
And the deep waters, darkly blue,
With funeral pace went marching through,
Opening two vistas. Upward far,
The flume fell twinkling like a star;
Downward, one long bright streak was seen,
Flashing 'twixt walls of living green.
Farewell, brave woods, the walks that shaded!
Since the rude axe your peace invaded;
Farewell, sweet vale! no more to brood
Recluse shall seek thy solitude.

The dusty highway ploughs thy breast;
The lumbering cart wheel breaks thy rest;
And in the solemn shades below,
Where May beheld the unmelted snow,
Ten times a day, through hill and dale,
With fifty freight cars at his tail,
A dragon black glides yelling through,
Soiling with dust the morning dew,
And from a throat that reeks with steam,
At thy green gate sends forth his scream,
Hideous to hear. O, never more
Shall time thy loveliness restore!

Yet why should I such fate lament,
Who, ere youth's dreamy days were spent,
Learned to foresee in each to-morrow
An equal chance for joy and sorrow.
'Tis sure small reason now for tears
That thou art changed in twenty years,
When I have known one single night
Snatch from my arms life's best delight.
I, too, am changed, nor more despair
Because things are not what they were,
Since with each change, howe'er bereft,
I count unnumbered blessings left;
And, prone to hope, I live at last
More in the future than the past.

Yet 'twould some pleasure yield, I ween,
Were I but master of life's stream,
As thou of thine, blue smiling river,
That flowest gaily still as ever.
In vain shall man his hands employ
All thy beauty to destroy;
Still in the groves thy steps are free;
He hath not locked thee there; I see
Thine untamed strength, delighting still
To sweep the vale and cleave the hill,
Where, laughing loud in joyous song,
Thou flashest the green fields along,
Till, in old Concord's battle plain,
Thy gladsome face grows grave again;
There, joined with Sudbury's sluggish tides,
In statelier march thy current glides.
Near that grey column, rude and low,[21]
Where Freedom's arm struck its first blow,
Thy reverential waters pass
Smooth as a lake of molten glass.
But here, fair stream, I heed thee not;
Flow on thy course, henceforth forgot.
Soon shalt thou hear amongst the hills
The clattering of an hundred mills,
There fated for some while to be
Tamed to a transient industry;
Trained to the trench to feed the flume,

Twirl the spindle, work the loom;
But tyrants cannot rein thee long;
Thou dost remember thine old song,
Which first was taught thee by the fountain
That fed thee on her native mountain;
Not long contented thus to be
Bound to a toilsome slavery,
Sudden thou leapest on the back
Of the mighty Merrimack,
Who bears thee on in laughing glee,
Glad of his new found company.
Soon shalt thou hear the surges roar
Where the great billows lash the shore;
There Neptune waits, and with delight
Sees his descendants heave in sight;
Alas! thou dost not know his face,
The kingly grandsire of thy race.
He was the father of the fountain
That first begat thee on the mountain.
'Tis done; old Newbury's sandbars crossed,
Soon shall the ship-lined shore be lost.
Farewell! the old sea king claims thy charms;
Thou'rt clasped in thy great grandsire's arms.

Lost for a while, thou shalt not perish;
Ocean's care thy life shall cherish;
And though thou seem like one entombed,
Not to dissolution doomed,

But exhaled, and soaring high,
Thou shalt mount the azure sky,
And to life eternal fated,
O'er and o'er shalt be created.
Sometimes in fierce torrents pouring,
When the winds and waves are roaring,
Thou, 'midst thunders bellowing loud,
Shalt leap in lightnings from the cloud;
Then in gentle showers of rain
Softly shalt descend again,
To refresh the thirsty earth,
And bring the buried flowers to birth.

Happy river! well in thee
May imagination see,
Mirrored, mortal destiny.
In alternate peace and strife,
Floweth thus the stream of life;
And what erring men call death
Is renewal of our breath;
Just as vapors from the main
Soar in mist, to sink in rain,
So in death life shall not rust,
But exhaled from worthless dust,
From earth's bosom it shall rise,
O'er again to greet the skies,
And its almighty Author bless,
Father of life and happiness.

Farewell, sweet Assabet! I see
Pictured in ocean, as in thee,
An emblem of eternity.

TO AN ALCHEMIST,

SEEKING THE ELIXIR OF LIFE.

AND would'st thou seek, misguided man,
To immortalize this earthly life?
A life, e'en now, whose little span
Suffices for unending strife.
O, spare thy labor, lest I see
Man's direst enemy in thee.

Full soon, e'en now, our years grow old;
Life's joys are spent before its breath;
And long before the blood grows cold,
The heart is oft consigned to death.
Should fate forget life's thread to sever,
Then guilt and grief would last forever.

Teach how to kill both time and care;
  Then will I hail thee as a friend;
But life will drive us to despair
  If Time himself must know no end.
O, curse not thou the race of men
With more than threescore years and ten.

If from the throats of one another
  Ye might so long their fangs restrain;
Where every wolf devours his brother,
  To make men happy still were vain;
For, all the fiercer passions past,
The beast turns miser at the last.

O, transient life of man! how vain
  Thy miserable days appear!
Record of guilt, despair and pain,
  Still lengthening on from year to year.
Ah, who would stay the hand of fate,
And give to woe an endless date?

I see the infant doomed to weep,
  Scared by a thousand causeless fears;
Life's happier half benumbed with sleep,
  The rest consumed in useless tears;
Wanting it knows not what, nor why,
Oft doubting if to laugh or cry.

The child his time in wishing wastes;
  Still building castles in the air;
The youth is restless till he tastes
  The cup whose waters breed despair;
Both weaklings, doomed full oft to stand
Misguided by another's hand.

I see the man, but as a child
  More shameless grown; he wastes life's hour
In aimless schemes or actions wild;
  Tormenting through abuse of power,
Tormented by his lusts, and torn
By passions of the Furies born.

I see the old man, self-wise and vain,
  Crabbed, and sour, and disappointed,
Cowardly and covetous; his frame
  Crazy and cracked, and all disjointed;
His wits unsound, his love unprized,
Despising youth, by youth despised;

And if extended to fourscore
  Upon life's rack, a lengthening train
Of bodily ills! What would'st thou more?
  Chill rheumatism's dull chronic pain,
Gravel and cramps, and twinging gout,
Rack the dry bag of bones about.

Then life goes back to its first tears;
  The dotard starves himself, in dread,
Forsooth, lest starve he may, and fears
  There's none will bury him when dead;
Nor dreams his heirs may well be tasked
With work they'll gladly do unasked.

Good God! beyond this living death
  Would'st thou have more? Thy search forbear;
Even let me earlier yield my breath,
  Following the gentle and the fair.
Since such is life, 'twas wisely sung,
" He in whom Jove delights dies young."

Good alchemist, e'en hold thy hand;
  Yield Death his due; hard lot 'twould be
If life's vast lazar house should stand
  Uncleansed to all eternity;
And if thou would'st control man's fate,
O shorten, not extend his date.

TO LUDOVICO CORNARO.

O THOU that for an hundred years
  Didst lightly tread the ancestral hall,
Yet sawest thy brethren bathed in tears,
  Cut down ere ripe, and round thee fall, —

Well didst thou deem long life the measure
  Of long enjoyment to the wise;
To fools alone devoid of pleasure;
  Thou would'st not die as the fool dies.

Robbed of thy titles, lands, and health,
  With man and fortune in disgrace,
In wisdom didst thou seek thy wealth,
  Thy peace, in friendship to thy race.

With thine eleven grandchildren met,
  Thou could'st at will become the boy;
And thine own sorrows to forget,
  Didst lose thyself in others' joy;

Could'st mount thy horse when past fourscore,
  And climb steep hills, and, on dull days,
Cheer the long hours with learned lore,
  Or spend thy wit on tales and plays.

In summer, thou wast friend of flowers,
And when the winter nights grew long,
And music cheered the evening hours,
Still clearest was the old man's song.

Thus, whilst thy calm and thoughtful mind
The ravages of time survived,
Three generations of mankind
Dropped round thee, joyless and short lived.

Thou sawest the flowers of youth decay,
Half dried and withered through excess,
Till nursed by virtue's milder ray,
Thy green age grew to fruitfulness.

Thou sawest life's barque on troubled seas
Long tossed; care's clouds thy skies o'ercast;
But calm content, with moderate breeze,
Brought thee to wisdom's port at last.

Life's evening, wherein most behold
Their season of regrets and fears,
Became for thee an age of gold,
And gave thee all thy happiest years.

As gentle airs and genial sun
Stay winter's march when leaves grow sere,

And when the summer's race is run,
 With a new summer crown the year;

So temperance, like that lingering glow
 Which makes the October woods so bright,
Did on thy vale of years bestow
 A glorious autumn of delight.

What useful lessons might our race
 From thy so sage experience draw!
Earth might become a joyous place,
 Would man but reverence nature's law.

Soar folly, self, and sense above;
 Govern each mutinous desire;
Nor let the sacred flame of love
 In passion's hurricane expire.

No wondrous works of hand or mind
 Were thine; God bade thee stand and wait,
A living proof to all thy kind
 That a wise man may master fate.

Happy that life around whose close
 The virtues all their rainbows cast;
While wisdom and the soul's repose
 Make age more blest than all the past.

ODE TO CONSCIENCE.

Mysterious monitor, that in the crowd
Art silent most, while other tongues are loud,
But in still seasons, when there's none to hear,
At night, and in lone solitudes, art near,
Startling the drowsy soul with speech severe!
O how shall he who fears thee from thee 'scape?
How learn to shun thee, thou that hast no shape?
If he would fly, the whirlwind thou outridest;
If he would hide, in his own heart thou bidest.
Who swiftest runs is soonest with thee met,
Remembering most when most he would forget.
If pleasure beckon, thou dost step between;
If business, thou on privacy wilt press;
If sleep beguile, thou hoverest in a dream,
Most dreadful in most absolute emptiness.
Knocking at no man's door, where thou wilt stay,
There enterest thou, nor wilt be driven away.

Sometimes in midnight dark thou dost mount
horse,
Riding fierce nightmare with thy fiend, Remorse;
Sometimes thou dost come sailing through the air,
Borne on the black wings of thy bird, Despair;
Yet ever without din,

Unseen thou enterest in,
Most like a voiceless breath,
When all is mute as death;
And he who hears thy still small voice
Reproaching, can no more rejoice;
And though he scour away in dread,
Soft as the step of thief, thy tread
His frighted fancy hears, and feels
Closely treading at his heels;
Or like one riding on his back,
Thou'rt with him though he shift his track;
And thy upbraidings, whispered clear,
Are ever ringing in his ear,
Like the continuous knell
Of never-ending bell.

When old Night her watch doth keep,
And the world is wrapped in sleep,
Flitting the eye and ear between,
Like a thing half heard, half seen,
Thou harpest on some dim remembered theme
Of evil, dead and buried long,
Which thou wilt weave in solemn song,
Recalling what we would remember not,
Making most clear what was most long forgot;
And in the breast
Breed such unrest

As one may note when some great wave's commotion
Sends its vast whispers from the heaving ocean.

No evil doth so hidden lie,
But thy keen sight can it descry,
And from the dark void of the past
Thou wilt draw out the thing at last,
Even as a dog brings stones that in the waves are cast,
And o'er and o'er the action will repeat,
And drop them reeking at his master's feet.
Or, as from deep earth out of sight
He drags a murdered corpse to light,
So from the guilty past thou drawest, unbid,
The thought that from its very self was hid,
And before blushing memory's eyes wilt lay
The hateful thing in the full glare of day.

Through stole and cassock thou canst see
The cold heart of hypocrisy;
Thou dost rend off the covering thin
From vanity's gay painted skin,
And what a virtue seemed, wilt show a sin.
Pride thou detectest in humility,
Fraud in sweet smiles, and selfishness canst see
In what the world deemed magnanimity.

The false, 'mid praise still hear thy voice condemn,
Saying, "Woe betide thy deeds; thou wouldst be
seen of men."

Names in thy thought do not for natures stand;
What men deem gold, to thee is glistering sand;
And whom the world calls fair, or just, or wise,
When tried by thee, thou dost so worthless prize,
That ugliness grows foul in its own eyes.

Who so just that can be sure
In thy judgment to stand pure?
Sole court whose verdicts none can doubt,
Setting our sins to find us out,
And dooming each, howe'er he err,
To be self-executioner,
Sure that the guilty will invent
Their own severest punishment,
And that no retribution will they lack,
So each be left to find the rod for his own back.

Thou restless one, begone, and sleep
In desert wild or forest deep;
In my heart why wilt thou lie,
Like a worm that will not die?
Why vex my unrefreshing slumber?
O'er and o'er my faults dost number;

And if I bid thee come no more,
Thou countest plainer than before.

Thou dost e'en creep into the house of mirth,
Hover unwelcome round the social hearth;
Oft in laughter wilt thou wail,
Make the rosy cheek turn pale,
And the affrighted soul wilt mock,
In the ticking of the clock;
Wilt in embers, while they die,
From the ashes seem to sigh.
Ever present where unsought,
Haunting each most secret thought,
With these harsh words wilt break our peace—
"Thou and thine evil soon must cease."
Even at the feast, in flowing bowl
Thou dost appal the guilty soul;
Wilt join the dance with noiseless tread,
And, with dull sighs and moanings dread,
Wilt mingle with the music's sweetest breath,
And change the gayest notes to the deep wail of death,
Bid lights burn blue, ghosts dance upon the wall,
And curtain every window with a pall.

But with a pang more fierce,
Thy vengeance loves to pierce

Their flinty hearts, whose selfish pride
Would human sufferings deride.
When some unwonted grief is brought to birth,
Shrouding in sudden gloom the joys of earth,
Then oft the wrong that they have done,
  While false prosperity protected,
Back upon themselves will come,
  Fierce, resistless, unexpected.

And oft, in hours of discontent,
When passion its last force hath spent,
Or when man's childish rage
Dissolves in hoary age,
And care no more can be forgot in jollity,
Thy frown can dotage fright from its frivolity.
Thou like a breaker from the past wilt roll,
And with sad memories overwhelm the soul,
And o'er thy surging waves the will hath no control.

The man, whose power oppressed the weak,
Whose face the humble durst not seek,
Ready to crush his rival, scourge his slave,
Yet by the world named chivalrous and brave,
Who, proud of lofty look and lordly eye,
Ne'er dreamed that insignificance could fly
To higher laws from human tyranny, —

He, who waxed fat in days of strength,
Reduced to helplessness at length,
Trembles with terror as he hears
Thy low voice whispering in his ears;
For thou wilt come in hour forlorn,
And him that laughed thy power to scorn
Thou wilt make sweat with fear and dread,
Even while he walks with towering head;
And while his countenance betrays
No signs of restless nights and days,
While in his pomp vain worldlings see
The bright smiles of prosperity,
Thou, lurking 'neath that outside gay,
Wilt lie concealed, and day by day
Gnaw peace, and hope, and health away.

Thou wilt even search that dullard out,
Who of his error lives in doubt;
Whose empty, undistinguished life
Is spent afar from noise of strife;
Who deems himself of saintly kind,
Since evil, lurking in his mind,
Ne'er into world-wide action grew,
Rejoices that his crimes are few;
Yet who, by sophistry acquitted,
Long did such evil as he durst;
A tyrant where the law permitted,

His enmities in secret nursed,
And, shrinking from the open blow,
Sought but to undermine his foe;
A wretch, who fain from danger's face would flee,
But never spared a prostrate enemy.
He did not murder, nor at midnight steal,
He ne'er rebelled against the common weal,
Was no adulterer, and detested dice;
Yet every virtue, springing from some vice,
Seems even sanctified in eyes of cowardice.
This man thanks God that he hath been
No profligate, like other men,
Since with less warmth, less love than they,
Less strong temptations led astray;
"Favored by grace!" as if Heaven's smile
E'er beamed benignant on the vile.

O thou, who with sharp eyes canst see
Each mean shift of hypocrisy,
Who, sparing oft the man of action,
Pitying the angry feuds of faction,
Art still most terrible to these,
Who would both God and mammon please,
Even though thou sleep, thou see'st, and wilt
awaken,
And judge; few e'er by thee are long forsaken.
Yes, thou wilt rouse, relentless even to them

Who not in action wronged their fellow-men;
Who pondered evil, but the deed refrained,
Who only wished, while chance or fear restrained.
Thou wilt disdain to ask, was crime committed?
Who but designed, or willingly permitted,
Hath done the deed, and may not go acquitted.
He starved the famished that refused him bread,
And he hath stolen who only coveted;
He stabs his victim who but hides the knife;
He slays his foe that will not save his life;
For 'tis the mind that murders, in thy sight;
The heart is guilty though the hands are white.
Man is deceived; he sees as in a dream,
Not what things are, but only what they seem.
He knows the act, but cannot judge the will.
The thief who walks in light loves darkness still;
Hatred can smile, hypocrisy can pray,
Silence can lie, embraces can betray;
And fraud, even with true words, from truth can
lead astray.
But thou wilt track imposture; thou wilt trace
Guile to the altar's self, and face to face
Wilt meet, and wilt unmask, reckless of time and
place.

Thou dost deem great what oft the world deems
least:

Fierce words, harsh thoughts, even cruelty to a beast,
The unnecessary blow, the wanton wound,
The shot that felled some creature to the ground,
That choked yon harmless wood thrush' music sweet,
And laid the songster lifeless at our feet;
Thou'lt ask by what right we have done such wrong,
Shattering God's beauteous instrument of song;
And when mischance, with some unwonted pain,
The wanton sport revenges not in vain,
Then these small wrongs will breed such melancholy
As health had laughed at for an idle folly.

All will come back; each creature's dying moan
Will haunt us with a sad, reproachful tone;
Things that seemed little in our eyes
Will grow in thought to monstrous size;
And faults for which we felt ashamed to care
Will, in the hour of anguish, breed despair.

O pitiless one, that would'st be sighing
In the dull ears of sick and dying,
Ever vexing most the breast
That hath greatest need of rest,

Wilt not thou, too, die at last
When the din of life is past?
Or, in the gloomy shades below,
Wilt thou forever to and fro
Pursue the viewless, voiceless band
That ghastly roams the Stygian strand?
Alas for man's poor, persecuted race,
If it shall ne'er escape thy tireless chase!
Might we but feel thy blows, thy countenance see,
'Twere comfort, even though vain from thee to flee;
But dreadful is the thought of unseen enemy.

Art thou, then, foe
To all men? No.
To them that are born blind,
Stern one, thou canst be kind,
Friend of the generous, just, and wise;
The upright alone with fearless eyes
Feel thine approach, and who can gain
Thy friendship may scorn earthly pain,
In desert wastes or prison cell
Need not discontented dwell,
Nor dread, if he but do thy will,
Them that the body only kill.
Even Error's self beneath thy sight
Walks guiltless, so he meant the right,

Even though unshocked and unrelenting
He hath stood by with mind consenting
To the destruction of the good;
And, though bestained with innocent blood,
Thou lettest him escape unchid,
Because he knew not what he did.
But, above all, is dear to thee
Plain truth and frank sincerity;
The wish benign, the action kind,
Ever a friend in thee will find.
Thou hast no care for human creeds,
Loving good will and generous deeds;
None ever yet with man dwelt as a brother,
But found thee kind and gentle as a mother;
    For thou, like God above,
    Ever best lovest love;
And thou and he will much forgive
To them that with much love shall live.
Whom thou befriendest ever walks in light;
His morn is not more lovely than his night;
Long, solitary years canst thou beguile,
Where thou wilt grant one fond, approving smile.

O when, 'neath wintry moonbeams pale,
Thou deignest thy dread face to unveil,
Or in dark night of storm to appear,
While none but dreary age draws near,

Let it not be with that sad look
At which repentant Peter shook
When the cock crew — that cheerless glance,
Which, keen and piercing as a lance,
Might make even Satan leer askance,
Met while on wicked errand bent;
Save that to be irreverent
Is the fixed nature of the devil,
Formed shameless to rejoice in evil;
If it so be that God could make
A spirit that delight could take
In doing ill for evil's sake,
Which surely were a monstrous thought.
Satan, I deem, his wrong hath wrought
Because the wight hath lived untaught,
An unweaned brat of Ignorance' brood,
Who never yet hath understood
To know the evil from the good.

Yet while thy face unveiled I see,
If thou should'st speak, let it not be
With such stern voice as, like a knell,
On ears of dying Judas fell,
When thou didst bid the wretch farewell;
But with approving smile and speech,
Such as of old could patience teach
To his grave master, on that morn
Which saw him unresisting torn

With bloody scourge and crown of thorn;
Or that sustained the steadfast mind
Of Belisarius, old and blind,
Who begged his bread with humble mien
Where once he had a conqueror been;
Or such as could sweet hope reveal
To virtuous Calas, doomed to feel
The terrors of the torturing wheel;
Or such as solaced Orleans' maid,
When, not in arms, but flames arrayed,
She met her sad fate undismayed;
Or such as in these later years,
Could nerve the hand and calm the fears
Of that fair girl of Normandy,
Who, with a dauntless soul and free,
Left home and friends, and, knife in hand,
Burning to save her ravaged land
From license, that, with ruthless tread,
Strode o'er the grave of freedom dead,
Flaunting her cap upon his head,
Slew, as she hoped, even in his den,
That dragon, gorged with flesh of men.
In vain; too numerous was the brood
Of savage beasts that raged for blood.

O, tranquil yet relentless power!
Reverenced even in childhood's hour,
Although some time from thee estranged,

I knew thee long with countenance changed;
Let me walk humbly in thy sight,
With honest thought, and heart upright.
None can avoid thee; though he fly
Beyond the realms of space, thine eye
Shall follow there, and all his ways descry.
If with forgetfulness to shun despair,
Listless he dwell, lo! thou art present there,
Still following like his shadow; who from thee
Hopes to escape, first from himself must flee.
Where'er I bide, thy still small voice I hear,
Accusing or excusing, ever near,
Judging my love, my hate, my hope, my fear;
Sifting e'en dreams, as well as thought and action,
Compacts dissolving, sundering the bands of faction.
With noiseless flight, thy spirit on viewless wings
Strengthens weak hands, and the strong arm unstrings,
Makes slaves go free, and can make slaves of kings.
Thou governest all— the sailor on the wave,
The soldier in his tent, the hermit in his cave,
The conqueror at his feast, the mourner at the grave.
Thou reignest in heaven, the archangels worship thee

Twin child with Love, first-born of Deity.
No seraph from thy face so far can fly,
But thou dost fix, and hold him with thine eye,
Wilt find him out in the most secret place,
Howe'er he turn, he must behold thy face;
Thou art o'er all, in all, throughout all time and
 space;
And if this earth, and the sweet light of day,
E'er in chaotic darkness melt away,
Thy deep low voice, 'mongst the celestial spheres,
Will still sound on throughout the unending years.
There wilt thou dwell the immortal hosts among,
Uttering thy runes severe in deathless song,
Falsehood from truth unravelling, right from wrong.

THE MORNING, NOON, AND NIGHT OF A SUMMER'S DAY.

MORNING.

Fair is the face of morn!
When, from his watch retreating, the day star
Sinks his pale lamp, and echoing hounds and horn
Ring o'er the hills afar;

When sleeps the cloudy fold,
Whose fleecy flocks o'er all the hills lie spread;
While, scarce concealed behind her veil of gold,
Aurora leaves her bed.

But when, with saffron locks,
From his cold bath upsprings the God of day,
All drenched in showers of light, the frightened flocks
Scatter in mists away.

Now, like a spark of fire,
His wheel above the plain begins to rise;
And now the flames, his chariot mounting higher,
Illumine all the skies,

Redden each rocky steep,
Spill down each slope, and fill with golden fire
The glen, the gorge, steal through the forest deep,
And wake each feathered choir.

Nor beauteous less, in days
When drifting fogs obscure the morn awhile,
Though oft, in mellow gleams, the silvery haze
Is softened to a smile.

Sometime, in vapory shroud,
The drizzly mists o'er all the meadows hang;

While, through the brooding rift, booms doubly loud
The distant clock tower's clang.

Soon from the valleys green
The reek, dispersed, floats drifting far and wide;
And now once more the pearly lake is seen,
Now the dark mountain's side.

And now the sudden blaze,
From yon blue rent, fires up the sparkling grass;
And as the God, unveiled, begins to gaze
Down in his watery glass,

Slowly from all the scene
The hoary vapors, high in heaven uprise;
And in blue hills, dark woods, and valleys green,
The boundless landscape lies.

NOON.

Sweet is the hush of noon!
When light hath searched each solitary nook,
And the brown oak scarce whispers to the tune
Of the light babbling brook!

When cattle on the hill,
Have gathered round the roots of each old tree;

Mute all, save the woodpecker's hammering bill,
Or buzz of humming bee.

When in the quiet wood
The turtles gather where the brook flows by;
All life retired to deepest solitude,
To shun the sultry sky;

Then in some grove forlorn,
Whose shade the bosom of the stream embowers,
'Mid glooms so deep that color sleeps unborn
In the night shrouded flowers,

'Mid twisted arch of leaves
Or beechen boughs, I also would retreat;
Or where the vine some drooping elm enwreaths,
A prostrate log my seat;

With book or friend retired,
Life's noise would I forget beside the rill,
Where calm content leaves nought to be desired,
Save to keep cool and still.

Yet wouldst thou covet more,
Seek wild Umbagog's chain of lakes where each
Opens its gate to each, till the far shore
Thy tired sight scarce could reach,

Save that, 'twixt slopes of green,
Through vistas blue thine eyes delighted stray
To where huge misty mountains bound the scene,
And soar in heaven away.

NIGHT.

Fair, too, is mellow eve!
When dusky shades o'er all the landscape creep,
And the bright clouds their rosy radiance leave
Upon the reddening deep;

When birds have ceased to sing,
And sleep in peace through all the drowsy vale,
And ghostly wraiths outstretch their vapory wings,
And up the meadows sail;

When living things seem dea
And dead ones to a dreamy life are born;
And shapeless visions sweep the air o'erhead,
Or walk the earth forlorn;

Till from her cloudy cave,
Comes out in silvery robes night's beauteous queen;
While each pale star peeps from his airy grave
Forth on the night serene.

But, hark! that bird I hear,
Which ever mourns at either end of day,
Chiding the stars, or whether they appear,
Or whether fade away.

Sweet day! morn, noon, and night!
Thou art all beautiful! through all thy range.
Thus let me ever deem thee; with delight
Viewing thine every change.

And, should that day arrive,
When nature can no longer make me gay,
May men regard me as no more alive,
And say, "He died that day."

THE RIVULET.

How merrily the streamlet flows,
Light prattling at my feet!
Now in a double track it goes,
And now its waters meet.
So changing oft from side to side,
Its floods now mingle, now divide.

Till to a river grown at last,
  Its currents part no more;
But blent in one, go journeying fast
  To swell old ocean's roar.
So did I deem, love's growing strength
Might of us two make one at length.

That we together, side by side,
  Might tread with equal pace;
Each other's joys and griefs divide;
  Till, having run life's race,
Commingling in Death's ocean wave,
We both might sleep in the same grave.

But no! our currents, sundered long,
  Flow on by different ways.
Thine to the east runs swift and strong,
  While mine far westward strays.
Each hies to reach a different main,
Nor more on earth shall meet again.

Farewell! till from Time's tides exhaled,
  We soar in upper skies;
And, from the source whence first we sailed,
  Once more together rise;
And born anew in summer's rain,
Flow on 'twixt banks of flowers again.

NEW YEAR'S WISH.

Companion of my heart, behold
How swift the seasons take their flight;
The new year overtakes the old,
As day treads on the steps of night.

Alas! my friend, no force of art
Can long arrest life's fleeting day;
The road divides where soon we part,
Each travelling to his house of clay.

Transient is all that hope would cherish;
Life stands upon destruction's brink,
Doomed in the arms of death to perish,
As light in evening's lap must sink.

Are the leaves fallen, the flowers decayed!
So friends, once many, fast grow few;
Life's sunshine darkens into shade;
Must life's affections perish too!

Must hearts long tried forget to blend!
Companions cease to know each other!
Must thou forget the name of friend,
And I thy faithful fondness, brother!

Nay, trust it not; 'twas God above
  Who bid our hearts harmonious beat;
He who himself is boundless love
  Shall find for love some calm retreat.

Yet, since the future is not ours,
  And all life's joys we briefly borrow,
Let kindness water friendship's flowers,
  Whose scent may haply sweeten sorrow.

As two good clocks in equal time
  Together click, nor slow nor fast,
Strike all the hours in even chime,
  Ringing together to the last,

So let our hearts, with faithful skill,
  In union beat till life shall end,
And, mingling with united will,
  Heed not time's weights as they descend.

THE HERMIT OF MELVERN WATER.

Two friendly travellers, side by side,
  Went forth to shun the city's noise;
One, thoughtful, pale, and gentle eyed,
The other flushed with manly pride —
    Both blithe as boys.

They journeyed many a weary mile,
  Each to the other like a brother;
They leaped the dyke, they climbed the stile,
Laughing and talking all the while
    With one another;

Until they reached the rocky glen
  Where Melvern waters foam and roar.
Here long ago, when younger men,
They'd roamed before — to roam again
    Now came once more.

The way with solemn shade was fraught,
  And for a while no words they spoke;
Each for some well known object sought;
Each mused, but neither told his thought,
    Nor silence broke.

Till when the hermit's hut they reach,
  Fixed in the mountain's deepest hollows,
Each to himself thus framed his speech —
The grave, the gay; but each from each
    Concealed what follows.

THE GAY.

There stands the ancient hermit man,
  Still dreaming lone beneath the hill
Where first his worthless life began;
There lives he yet; he hath no plan,
    An idler still.

He moves as if he were in doubt
  Which way to go, and 'mongst the trees
For squirrel holes he hunts about,
Sees some go in and some come out —
    Smiles as he sees.

Thus, crutch in hand, he jogs alone,
  Now stops on silly flowers to pore,
Now with his staff he strikes a stone,
Now moralizes on a bone,
    But nothing more.

Thou selfish soul! 'tis life's abuse
  To spend thy time in such a way,

Thy dreams are but a poor excuse
For one who might have been of use
In his long day.

THE GRAVE.

The second mused: O, hermit sage,
Who, wearied with man's loveless strife,
And sick of the world's vassalage,
Hast here retired to spend thine age —
An envied life!

Thou seemest youthful as a boy,
Whilst gazing with so sweet a smile;
And though thy hands find small employ,
Yet in this dull world to enjoy
Is worth life's while.

When all our idle lives are o'er,
Whoe'er can say he hath done as much,
Need scarcely for lost time deplore;
Nine tenths of all the world, and more,
Do worse than such.

THE GAY.

In his dark log house, low and mean,
With no companion but a cat,
He on his daily bread grows lean,

While she her daily mouse picks clean,
Half starved at that.

Yet still she follows at his heel,
Purrs and sits by him like a wife
Honest she is — there's nought to steal;
Courts not the fire — there's none to feel;
Such is their life.

No neighbors near his joys enhance;
No faithful friend his arms receive;
No wife, no babes, to greet his glance;
No village children come to dance,
And bless his eve.

No music cheers his hours forlorn,
Save when some bullfrog's croak he hears;
Or when from early eve till morn,
The shrill mosquito winds her horn,
Full in his ears.

Sad fate, to dwell like one that's dead,
Unknown except to wolf or fox,
Or woodpecker, that taps o'erhead,
Or wildcat, that, with stealthy tread,
Prowls 'mongst the rocks.

I'd rather drown me in the sea,
  Than dwell in such a cheerless gloom.
Sure, man was made with man to be,
To live in sweet society,
    Not in the tomb.

THE GRAVE.

Ah, what a blessed life, I ween,
  'Mongst harmless birds to live like one!
No bickerings blight the peaceful scene;
No blood bestains the herbage green;
    Hated by none

Silent he wanders; day by day,
  Bent on God's glorious works to brood,
Where harmless conies skip and play,
Fearless and free, and far away
    From black ingratitude.

More blest than he who lives unknown
  'Midst jostling crowds, and finds no brother;
Town on all sides, yet ne'er a home;
Where each lives for himself alone,
    None for another.

THE GAY.

I've seen him stroll with thumb-worn book
 At least five miles from any house;
And for whole hours he'll stand and look
In the bright waters of the brook,
 Still as a mouse.

Sure no Narcissus glances back
 On that dark skin and visage weird,
Which almost turns the waters black.
How hooked his nose! how crooked his back!
 What frowzy beard!

THE GRAVE.

Lovely to see in streamlet fair,
 Wisdom beholding its own face.
Gleams back no hatred, no despair;
Smiles only are reflected there,
 And virtue's grace.

THE GAY.

What an unthrifty life he leads!
 But one small patch of beans and pease!
He plants a few poor garden seeds,
His radish beds are full of weeds,
 His own, of fleas.

He hath no silver and no gold,
  All kinds of wealth, all power doth lack;
No house, no barns, no crops, no fold,
Not even a cloak, to keep the cold
    From his old back.

To live in such a lonely state,
  Like some wild creature in its hole,
And be content with such a fate,
This to my mind doth indicate
    A grovelling soul.

THE GRAVE.

Divided still 'twixt thought and toil,
  This man I deem most truly wise.
He wastes no words, he spends no oil,
And all he wants the fruitful soil
    Each day supplies.

He fears no loss, he feels no cares;
  Hath no false friends, no foes to dread;
No crafty knaves here set their snares;
No creditors, nor hungry heirs
    Grudge him his bread.

No passions to disturb repose, —
  No fear of war, wind, wave, or fire, —

His placid life in calmness flows
'Midst gentle showers, and silent snows,
        Without desire.

THE GAY.

In this rich world to have no choice;
    With none to help, with none to love,—
What joy is this! where none rejoice;
There's none to listen to his voice,
        Save God above.

And if he mourn, there's none to cheer,
    And when he dies, there's none to weep.
His bones, unwatered by a tear,
Must bleach ungraved; there's no one near,
        To mark his sleep;

Unless perhaps the wolf or crow,
    That dragged his corpse 'mongst yonder stones,
For some brief time his fate might know,
Till drifting leaves and drizzly snow
        Enwreathe his bones.

THE GRAVE.

No false opinions here divide;
    In friendly peace live man and brute:
He and his cat are of one side,

And were they not, the world is wide ;—
    There's no dispute.

And if he's sick, no man of skill
  Shall come to thump and to explore,
With purge and plaster, drop and pill,
To order things but as God's will
    Ordered before.

The thought of death will breed no fear,
  He'll wait his tap with a mind steady.
A trifling change it will appear
To one who was so long, while here,
    Half dead already.

No base dependants shall embrace,
  Nor brew with pungent drugs mock tears;
No canting priest, with lengthening face,
Shall preach of the soul's hopeless case,
    To dying ears.

Nor bustling relatives draw nigh,
  To shrug, with imitated dread;
Or with false tongue and long drawn sigh,
Exclaim, "Pray God he may not die!"
    Yet wish him dead.

And when life's worn and crazy mill
  Hath shut her gate, and slacked her wheel,
No curious throngs the house shall fill,
To hear the reading of his will,
    Longing to steal.

No funeral guests the train shall swell,
  To bear him back to nature's womb,
'Midst tramp of feet, and toll of bell;
Nor in rich garments shall he dwell,
    In a foul tomb.

But midst these hills and forests wild
  His aged eyes in peace shall close;
Death shall approach with manner mild,
And take him as one bears a child
    To sweet repose.

And while his shroud pale winter weaves,
  Summer with showers his limbs shall lave;
Autumn shall line his bier with leaves,
And twine her many colored wreaths
    To grace his grave.

Then shall my thoughts the sage revere,
  Who nature viewed with loving eyes;

Content to live on homely cheer,
Regarding with delight sincere
God's earth and skies.

And now they reached the pathway bar;
Leaped o'er; but neither spoke his mind.
The hermit's pool gleamed back afar,
In distance twinkling like a star,
Their path behind.

Each turns to look once more, and sees
The lean old man far down the hill,
His white locks waving in the breeze;
And at the squirrels in the trees
He gazes still.

THE SOLITARY MAN.

What dost thou there alone
Seated on mossy stone,
Intent to view the flowery ground,
And grassy hassocks scattered round,
Or half asleep beside the murmuring rill,
To watch the cattle feeding on the hill?
Thine eyes have gazed all day, yet have not seen their fill.

An idler thou, I'm told,
Sad, solitary, cold;
A man, they say, who hath few friends,
Who little gives and nothing lends,
And lives alone; men sneering pass thee by,
And yet, old man, methinks I can descry
Somewhat humane and wise within thy clear,
gray eye.

'Tis true, the proud, the great,
Disdain thy low estate;
They lawfully that rob the poor,
And scorn the humble, call thee boor.
Perhaps yon factor, deaf to sighs and prayers,
Yon usurer grown lean to feed his heirs,
Deem worthless one like thee, who only dreams
and bears.

Honest thou art and civil,
Dreading nor man nor devil.
No patron hast thou in the great,
Why shouldst thou care for church and state?
None knocking at thy door I ever see,
Save those that come for taxes, tithes, or fee.
Why, since thou'rt nought to men, should men be
aught to thee?

Yet this, old man, thou provest,
Them that love thee thou lovest,
Or else thou wert not there alone,
So long upon thy mossy stone,
Plainly so full of joy, from morn till night,
Gazing on nature's face with such delight,
That I feel friendly grown with thee, even at the sight.

The sighing breezes woo thee,
The light brook babbles to thee,
The fearless squirrels round thee leap,
And birds come singing thee to sleep:
The shagbarks their ripe nuts around thee shed,
While whispering oaks and murmuring pines o'erhead,
To make thy couch more soft, the earth with dry leaves spread.

The conies, clustering near,
Sport round thee without fear,
And clouds of crows, that round thee rise,
Respect thy sleep and spare thine eyes.
Each dumb thing here regards thee as a brother;
Nature alone hath been to thee a mother;
Therefore thou lovest her as thou dost love none other.

The scenes that charm thee here
Were to thy childhood dear.
Thy youth, thy manhood here were spent,
And age here found thee still content;
Yon grave claims all thy tears, these fields thy pride;
Thy loved ones in yon cottage lived and died;
Each rock, each tree, hath some fond feeling sanctified.

O, lone one, thou dost teach
This doctrine without speech,
That man in much is sport of chance;
That accident and circumstance
Our lives control; that past associations
Form of our good and evil the foundations;
These elevate and these depress both men and nations.

Who would judge men, must learn
If chance were kind or stern;
Nature and habit, not reflection,
Direct in most the soul's affection;
To know the man we must have known the boy,
The sources of his sorrow and his joy;
Harsh judgments both our own and others' peace destroy.

Our thoughts, even as our laws,
Judge acts, but not the cause.
We view with a contemptuous face
Men not of our own creed or race.
Nature hath made man's bitterest foe his brother,
And custom, siding with our partial mother,
Widens still more the breach that parts us from each other.

All ignorant of God's will,
Man is presumptuous still.
A narrow judge of good and evil,
He this one angel names, that devil;
Though some, not bad, hard fate hath forced astray;
And some, not good, were saints deemed in their day;
A destiny hath shaped our lives, even as our clay.

He learns in an ill school,
That scorneth even the fool;
Both, on life's sea are doomed to float
As messmates in a leaky boat;
Bound to some goal unknown, the wise asks where,
His question answered is by empty air;
The fool, with cheerful face, glides on and doth not care.

The one, with haughty looks
Points to his musty books,
And cries with a contracted brow,
Stand off, I better am than thou;
But God, the infinitely good and wise,
Pities them both, forbearing to despise;
Both are as fools alike in his all-seeing eyes.

He, who in narrow bound,
Hath life's experience found;
Ne'er summoned to affairs of state,
Or on grave things to meditate;
Who finds his love, his hate, his hope, his fear,
All in a little hamlet; yet e'en here
May prove a soul sublime, though in a narrow sphere.

Each hath a destined lot,
By self determined not;
The base oft born to rule a nation;
The princely soul to humble station;
The king himself may die at last a boor.
The wise philosopher finds nothing sure,
Save a calm, steadfast mind, to the upright and pure.

Some, born to high estate,
Have been by unkind Fate
So cramped, that spiders, toads, and flies,
Grew dear companions in their eyes.
There have been men, who, made with healthy sight,
Have had their day so long obscured by night,
That they have learned at last in darkness to delight.

There have been men sincere,
Whose lot was so severe,
That they have lost that joy in others,
We feel for parents, friends, and brothers;
But yet with loathsome things delighted grew;
For love is still life's want, as Plutarch knew,
Who said, they seek the false, who have not found the true.[22]

Yet he, who cat or dog
Can love, so far loves God.
'Tis a good shepherd loves his fold;
Hypocrisy alone is cold.
And who, shut out from man, his life hath spent,
Yet to his herds hath been benevolent,
Enjoys, though in a low degree, God's own content.

How much more fool than thou,
Yon wight with wrinkled brow,
Who to all science makes pretension,
Yet love's blest art of self-extension
Ne'er yet conceived; who seeks the health's protection
Rather in drugs, prescribed with grave direction,
Than in a heart, which feels for all God's works affection.

Even they that call thee cold,
Less love mankind than gold;
Where in the haunts of social life,
Bound but by fellowship of strife,
They spend their days reviling and reviled.
The worldling loves but self in his own child,
And thought's sweet solitudes he deems a pathless wild.

Yet none hate truth or right;
Even they that shun the light,
Look wistful back toward virtue's star;
The good themselves, forsooth! how far
From perfect goodness! yet from age to age
Truth still advances, and earth's wisest sage
Needs with each generation a new pupilage.

Poor soul! thy narrow mind,
By narrow views confined,
Ne'er soared beyond thy little field,
And history's book to thee is sealed.
Thou lovest that which lies about thy door,
And best, whate'er thou hast loved best of yore;
So art a faithful friend; pray how canst thou be
more?

The patriot, sacred name!
No merit more can claim;
He to a greater interest clings,
Whilst thou art true to trifling things;
But at his country's bound he makes his stand,
For her alone he lifts his voice or hand;
He cares not what befalls men of another land.

Yet larger love of men
Hath the world-citizen.
He moves within a wider sphere,
And all mankind to him are dear.
He, who the men of many climes hath known,
Finds virtue's flowers in other lands have grown;
While he who stays at home, all goodness deems
his own.

But who, with calm delight,
Views through his glass at night
The silent heavens, and sees the skies
All twinkling with ten thousand eyes;
And deems each one a living world to be;
He'll scarce be bound to earth; his love would flee
To dwell with distant stars in loving harmony.

While God, who from on high,
Holds all things in his eye,
From the vast chain of circling spheres,
To the small orbs of human tears,
To such an infinite sympathy expands,
His charity all space, all time, commands,
And loves the world the more, since wrought by his own hands.

Good soul! still all alone,
Muse on thy mossy stone.
Why should I thy sweet peace deride?
Still watch thy cows; the world is wide;
And if I e'er mount nearer heaven than thou,
This is my shame, to wear a cloudy brow,
Whilst thou art worshipping as well as thou knowest how.

Nay, even yon hare hard by,
Who cannot look more high
Than the green herbs that brush his nose,
Cropping the fresh leaves as he goes,
Hath also his religion, and I fear,
His pleasure to pure worship comes more near,
Than upturned eyes, long prayers, and looks austere.

THE RAILROAD TRAIN.

FIRST TREATMENT.

What war-ship through the valley rides,
Blazing afar 'midst fog and thunder ?
Now o'er the hills in air it glides,
Now dives the lofty mountains under.
How fast she flies, by fiery tempests fanned,
Filled by whose breath her smoky sails expand,
And bear her proudly on o'er oceans of dry land.

Hath sea-god, or enchanter's wand
Thus driven thee from thy native main,
In such hot haste to invade the land,
And cast thy anchors on the plain ?

Yet now no ship of war thou seem'st to be,
But some rich argosy from Indian sea,
By favoring gales impelled, and freighted weightily.

Thy long train, like a fleet of boats,
Moves upon many a shining keel;
Each on a magic river floats,
By wizard spells transformed to steel.
And now they skim the fields 'midst clouds of soot,
Now swim the stream, now through the gorge they shoot,
To reach their inland port, even at the mountain's foot.

Down from the hills I see thee sail,
And joined by mates from every side,
Each, by a self-created gale,
Drives swiftly on to reach the tide.
Freighted with trunks of many a tree,
And from a grassy to a watery sea,
Bearing as by free will, the works of industry.

And to those same hills bringing back
The gathered wealth of distant climes;
Each beacon light from mast of black
Now through a dusty tempest shines;

And now 'mongst billowy rocks their sails expand;
And now their bright keels spurn the desert strand,
To plough through flinty spray, o'er bays of glittering sand.

THE RAILROAD TRAIN.

SECOND TREATMENT.

WHAT fiery steed comes clattering past,
With reeking breath and streaming mane?
His snort is like the wintry blast,
His flight outstrips the hurricane.

Breathless he pants, yet seems to sail,
With such smooth force he cuts the wind.
There, like a dragon's, glides the tail,
Outstretched a full half mile behind.

And now the huge beast checks his speed,
And stops to drink at yonder trough,
And on his meal of logs to feed;
And now once more, with husky cough,

He starts afresh, and, whinnying loud,
  Pierces the air with shrilly neigh ;
Now, like the lightning from a cloud,
  Flashes amongst the hills away.

I hear him still, though out of sight,
  Through the cleft mountain thundering on ;
Now a thin wreath of misty white
  Curls o'er the hill top, and he's gone.

Hark from afar that piercing scream !
  From five miles off he bids farewell.
Such speed will bear the fiend, I ween,
  Ere nightfall to his native hell.

Such yon poor Indian's wish, no doubt,
  Who hears from far the frightful sound,
And fears lest he shall be cast out
  Ere long from his last hunting ground.

Well might he dread thy voice to hear,
  Who deemed thee by man's hand untrained,
Free thine own reckless course to steer,
  And scatter mischief unrestrained.

Thy head erect and hide of black
  Oft fill the unwonted swain with dread.

The scared flocks scamper from thy track,
Wild beasts in terror hear thy tread,

And to more secret shades take flight,
When thou through dark com'st rumbling nigh,
While, fitful breathing on the night,
The fire sparks from thy nostrils fly.

Yet, sooty monster, such alone
Have cause to fear; for through all time,
Of all philanthropists, not one
Can prove beneficence like thine.

Thou, sea to sea, and land to land,
And state to state dost firmly bind.
Through thee shall earth and ocean stand
In a more steadfast friendship joined.

Thou hastenest news of good and ill,
And scatterest knowledge in thy flight.
Through thee shall man's industrious skill
Earth's hidden treasures bring to light.

By thee made tame, each jarring race
Its old hostilities shall quell.
Thou shalt subdue both time and space,
And dark delusion's mists dispel.

O swift-winged Messenger, or whether
  A thinking or a thoughtless thing,
That thus so speedily together
  The tribes of all the earth canst bring,

Till through repeated intercourse,
  Men are more friendly grown each day!
Well may we thank, O iron horse,
  The chief who taught thee to obey;

Who noosed thee in thy native wild,
  And tamed thy rage with patient skill,
And made thee gentle as a child,
  The servant of a wiser will.

But see, — he slacks his pace at length,
  And answers shrill his master's call,
And slowly drags his giant strength,
  With noisy raptures, to his stall.

There rest until the groom at morn
  Shall harness thee to early toil,
With a hot breakfast make thee warm,
  And rub thy stiffened joints with oil.

Then tackled to thy task once more,
  Upon thy destined journey press,

And make the joyful mountains roar;
  Give voice to the lone wilderness,

Where drowsy Echo startling wakes,
  And cheers thee on with deafening screams;
While from thy nostrils the hot flakes
  Sweep o'er her hill in fiery streams.

THE MOUNTAIN JOURNEY.[23]

Reader, hast thou e'er sought to gain
  The summit of some giant hill,
When all thy comrades toiled in vain,
  Though firm of foot and strong of will,
Gave up their purpose in despair,
And left thee lonely climbing there?

Sometimes the tangled pathway wound
  O'er narrow ridge or dizzy steep,
Where oft the frail and slippery ground
  Forced thee on hands and knees to creep,
And from the precipice's brink,
Oft threatened 'neath thy feet to sink.

Sometimes before thine eyes uprose
  Majestic slopes, dark robed in firs,
Which on all sides the prospect close,
  In stately amphitheatres,
While down their sides each cataract pale
Glows like some distant comet's tail.

No poisonous shrub of sickly hue [24]
  Mounts from the plain to meet us here,
But gold, and red, and heavenly blue
  Smiling along the path appear.
Surely thou saw'st, with deep surprise,
The road so fair to reach the skies!

But passed the pine and birchen grove,[25]
  The scene begins to grow less gay;
The trees that swept the skies above
  Now dwindle, and next die away;
Till, of all other growth bereft,
The stunted firs alone are left.

A squalid, straggling, rigid band
  Of aged dwarfs around thee stood,
Such as of old, in fairy land,
  Oft dwelt beneath the enchanted wood;
Some seen from caves sly peeping out,
While some the hillside strolled about.

But soon in line the dwindling host
  Stands right across thy path, thick set,
Where each, firm planted at his post,
  Receives thee with fixed bayonet.
That hope forlorn, who would subdue,
Must climb the ranks, for none break through.

And lastly, nought thine eyes behold
  Save blasted stocks that gird thee round,
A treeless waste, where breezes cold
  Sweep o'er the bleached and shrubless ground.
Didst thou not deem such thriftless soil
But ill repaid thy weary toil?

Yet, on the landscape looking round,
  What splendid prospect meets the eyes,
Where, steep, and high, and hoary crowned,
  A thousand mountains round thee rise,
Each gazing o'er some neighbor's head,
In ranks on ranks unlimited!

And now 'tis but a dreary route,
  Rocky, and wild, and wasted all;
And clambering slow, thou'rt oft in doubt,
  Or whether thou shalt stand or fall;
Whilst clouds encompassing the way,
Sometimes obscure the light of day;

Sometimes are changed to silvery dew,
  When sunlight bursts their folds of gray,
Glances the grizzly spectres through,
  Or gilds their wings with glittering ray;
Sometimes the storm king bellowing loud,
Shoots at thee from the darkest cloud.

Here thy last comrade turns about,
  And downward gropes his drizzly way;
Thou ploddest still, till, with a shout,
  Thy glad eyes pierce that veil of gray,
And gazing through the cloudy reek,
Behold the mountain's topmost peak.

'Tis reached, and the pleased eye explores
  What glorious, soul-enchanting scene!
Far, far below, the tempest roars,
  Above, the blue heavens smile serene;
Whilst snow-white blossoms round thee blow,
Thine eyes had never seen below.

Around thy feet thou seest no trace
  Of the green land thou late didst leave;
All new! the very insect race [23]
  Are strangers to the vales beneath;
And the fair flowers that round thee grow
Have left their friends in lands of snow.

And as the clouds beneath thy feet[27]
Their dark folds open now and then,
Thou seest the driving rain storm beat
Upon the lower world of men,
Whilst thou, enthroned in heaven's high arch,
Behold'st, unmoved, the tempest's march.

O say, if afterward this thought
Ne'er struck thee, amongst wrangling crowds?
So virtue's path with storms is fraught;
The way to truth is veiled in clouds;
And he, who would their glories view,
Must strain his strength, and struggle through.

Weary and faint, without a friend,
And guideless, must he travel still,
The journey, rugged till its end,
But beauteous flowers crown all the hill.
And to reward him for the past,
His peace shall perfect be at last.

Like them that climb the mountain's height,
He, from a firm, but rocky seat,
Beholds far down delusion's light,
From error's clouds, that 'neath him sweep,
Darting through storms its vivid flash,
Followed by passion's thunder crash.

12

Yet o'er the tempest raised secure,
He, lordly throned in worlds serene,
Looks, from a cloudless sky and pure,
Upon the wild, distracting scene,
As calmly as his eyes survey
The sunset of a summer's day.

TO A LEARNED MAN DREADING THE APPROACH OF OLD AGE.

And dost thou grieve, because old age
Comes travelling on so fast?
And that life's weary pilgrimage
Must wear thee out at last?
Do wrinkled brows and locks of gray
Thy troubled fancy fright?
The sun hath beamed on all thy day—
Why dread the moon at night?

No, let the bad, the vain, the weak,
The flight of time regret,
In pleasure's ranks who vainly seek
Their errors to forget.

Who tares have planted in the past
  Must in the future pine;
Who forced in spring life's flowers too fast
  Must mourn in harvest time.

But thou, that on grave wisdom's track
  Hast gleaned such precious store,
And on life's highway looking back,
  Seest little to deplore,
Down to the vale of years may'st wend
  Thy way, and smile at care;
'Tis what we have been, valued friend,
  That makes us what we are.

He, who in folly's train hath danced,
  Or lived the slave of gain,
Who ne'er another's joy enhanced,
  Nor soothed another's pain,
The envious man whose heart impure
  Corrodes within his breast, —
Of all the miseries such endure,
  Decrepitude's the least.

But wise old age, more blest than youth,
  Through error's mists can see,
And, having faithful been to truth,
  From prejudice is free;

The quiet mind resists decay,
  And still is health's defence;
It thaws the frosts of time away
  By sweet benevolence.

And as the late sun, glowing bright,
  Melts on the ocean's breast,
And casts his glory half the night
  O'er all the reddening west,
So virtuous age sinks calmly down,
  Refulgent to the last,
And leaves the light of worth's renown
  To beautify the past.

THE EXPERIENCED PHILOSOPHER.

HIS REPROOF OF THE WISH TO COMMENCE LIFE ANEW.

How has thy life been spent, that in those years,
  When time should hail thee master, thou would'st still
Tread backward to the senseless age of tears,
  To be once more the slave of others' will,
And live a creeping, weeping, cowering thing,
Rather than crown thyself, o'er self, a king?

What art hath childhood or to soften fate,
Or force subdue?—reason with will at strife.
And wouldst thou fly from thought to thoughtless state?
Ah! brief at best the years of rational life!
Full soon shall dreary dotage seal each sense
In a dull, fretful, drivelling impotence.

Yet, if to 'scape from sorrow thou would'st fly
From life's gray, sober landscape, to the green,
E'en children too are doomed full oft to cry,
The cause though light, the suffering is as keen.
Sorrows, like dogs, will track us till we die—
The only friends of man that ne'er will fly.

Or dost thou long in loving arms to rest
From labor and a self-dependent state?
Or art thou friendless? the fond nurse's breast
Seems for the child, more miserable fate,
Since, for the rapture of a fond caress,
It pays the penalty of helplessness.

Dost thou lament thine errors, fain once more
At life's first source thy virtue to renew?
Will childhood thy lost innocence restore?
Thou changest evening damps for morning dew.
Yon fretful babe might tell thee, could it speak,
In this consists its innocence—'tis weak.

Rather rejoice that time hath set thee free
From blind obedience to each tyrant fool,
Whether to nurse or parent it may be,
Or to the petty despot of a school,
Who oft with misspent toil life's field prepares,
And scatters wide the seeds of future tares.

Yet, art thou fond of servitude, mankind
Will scarcely fail to enslave thee, chaining down
Thy faith to false opinion, till the mind
Less loves the truth than fears the false world's frown.
Masters enough will bind thee, soul and sense,
Till reason claim thy sole obedience.

But would'st thou truly be renewed, even now,
As chemic art can change the natural night
To greater than noon's brightness, so may'st thou
Life's waning hours illume with moral light,
Whose influence mild shall cheer thy latest day,
And keep thee all unwasted by decay.

Come then; and first, if thou life's art would'st learn,
Keep thy neglected body in good health,
Or truth thy jaundiced eyes shall scarce discern.
Next, knowledge seek, which can bestow such wealth

As thou from prowling thief need'st ne'er conceal ;
Nor moth, nor rust, nor Time himself shall steal.

Next be thou cheerful ; nor let sullen eyes
  Scatter black clouds to darken all life's joy ;
The proud, the envious, and the seeming wise,
  By frowns their own and others' peace destroy.
But cherish Hope, of placid Temperance born,
Who reins life's sun within a lingering morn.

Next be humane, and with no evil eye
  Look on thy fellows ; hatred's glance can chill
The warmest sunbeam of life's morning sky ;
  While love, care's darkest day with light can fill,
And 'gainst the night of age make sure defence
With the soft moonlight of benevolence.

Nor ever wander far from Reason's side,
  And walk with Truth as with a bosom friend ;
With these, and Love divine, thy life divide,
  And wait in blest tranquillity thine end ;
Not hurried madly on by passion's blast,
But warmed with virtue's sunshine to the last.

So may'st thou live undazzled by the light
  Of vain delusion ; Fancy near shall stand,
But as thy handmaid, ever in thy sight,

To wait and serve thee, never to command.
Thus shalt thou quite surmount men's foolish fears,
Lord of thy pleasures, passions, and ideas.

In short, — be perfect; for the race of men
Shall ne'er o'ermaster evil till that day
When God it copies; 'twill discover, then,
No tyrant's will hath forced it to obey.
Men will love truth, as God loves to be just;
'Tis best — the only reason why they must.

And when thou hast advanced to that last bound,
Where Reason's self her way hath lost in light,
While worlds, in order circling round and round,
Confirm thy faith in an all-ruling right,
Then wisely may'st thou thine old wish restore
To be on earth a little child once more.

Yet not the child that frets with fruitless tears,
Doomed like a reptile on the ground to crawl,
But one that shall be master of the years,
Hoping all things, enduring, trusting all,
And bound to all by the great law of love —
Wise as the serpent, harmless as the dove.

Then shalt thou reverence rightly, when thy mind
Feels this vast world so little in its thought,

And God unlimited; then will it find
  The cause of Wisdom's boast, that she knows
      nought;
And fold its wing, content henceforth to see
All this vast world a boundless mystery.

Then shalt thou in true charity delight,
  Last of its wants which the sick soul discovers;
Here fools and wise may truthfully unite
  In one conclusion — that they both are brothers.
Fools nothing know, but fail to find it out;
The wise that they know nothing feel no doubt.

TO THE MEMORY OF WASHINGTON.

O, WISE of counsel! with unseemly speech
  Men still describe thee, though thy worth they
      know;
And ranking thee with heroes, yet would teach
  That thou wast great but by not being so ·
As if than wisdom aught can greater be,
More perfect aught than perfect symmetry.

Some would deny thee genius, friend of right,
  Since with firm will thy passions thou could'st
      sway;

Such genius deem but some erratic light,
That darts across the heavens, and dies away;
Fond of the strange, these think the master mind
Must needs be something of the monstrous kind.

But 'tis distorted objects seem most great.
Thus hunchback dwarfs, though scarce a cubit high;
While Antwerp's proudest fane men underrate,
Whose lofty pinnacles transfix the sky.
Just forms appear not bulky to our eyes,
While shapes uncouth seem swelled to monstrous size.

So distance cheats. The mountain viewed from far
Seems low; experience wise seems mean to youth;
Small, to the naked eye, each distant star;
Dark, to the ignorant mind, the light of truth.
Fools deem them weak that godlike wisdom teach;
All things seem least that lie most out of reach.

By the same law, the vain and narrow mind,
Skilled in one art, will noisiest praise command.
Most to the greater beautiful are blind,
Despising where they do not understand;

Earth's wisest sage a weakling seems to such;
They deem him nought because he knows so much.

O, just man, whom thy countrymen name father!
  No common type can I behold in thee;
Like some colossal statue art thou rather,
  Standing alone in simple majesty,
So well proportioned that the common eye
In thee could but a common man descry,
Save that to reach thee it must look so high.

THE SOUL'S INVOCATION.

A GLANCE DOWN THE RIVER OF LIFE INTO THE OCEAN BEYOND.

MASTER unknown, whose power divine
Upon the restless floods of time
Hath launched my bark and spread my sail,
While, swiftly driven before the gale,
My keel glides on! I feel thy breath
Impel me toward the straits of death,
Beyond whose narrow pass my soul
Beholds the billowy ages roll,
But sees no end; there Fancy's eye
Through the dim distance can descry

Only dense vapors, wastes profound,
A world of waters, and no bound.
Fate flies before, and I behind,
Her wings, outstretched upon the wind,
O'ercloud the skies, and rushing fast,
Each landmark sweeps into the past.
Upon the river's banks, each day,
Life's ever-changing flowers decay;
And as the gardens of delight
On either margin heave in sight,
My bark so swiftly shoots ahead,
Scarce can I look ere all is fled.
The verdant shores behind me glide;
Each hour the river grows more wide;
And now the castles of Despair,
With frowning towers, rough, bleak, and bare,
Loom from the desolate wastes of care.
I see gay Pleasure's wingéd train
Cleaving the gale above the main;
The wedgéd phalanx, high o'erhead,
Soars on its course, all backward sped
To greet the spring on youth's green shore,
A land I must behold no more.
Now in the mist it melts away,
Shrunk to a speck of dusky gray,
Now lost in clouds. O, beauteous day!
I see thy sun, which rose like gold,
Set in the distance, pale and cold.

The shades of night around me creep;
The fogs come drifting o'er the deep;
Fain would I turn my prow; 'tis vain;
The current drives me toward the main,
Never, ah, never to return again!

Through all my route, and shining clear,
A row of lighthouses appear;
One at the boundaries of each year,
Whose moving lantern ceaseless burns,
Where every season glows by turns:
Now the green lights of spring appear;
Now summer's gold is shining clear;
Now autumn gleams with purple hue,
Now the dull blaze of wintry blue;
And as each beacon light is past,
Another, turning like the last,
Glares on the wave; and as I go,
Each glides behind me, till the row
Dwindles at last to two or three —
Beyond, illimitable sea.
Now, at the last revolving light,
The gray expanse grows dark with night;
I see the fast-receding shore;
I hear the distant breakers roar;
And soon, on greater billows tossed,
Like one who hath some causeway crossed,

I see the glowing path behind,
With its long row of lanterns lined;
Where the lights blend their colored rays,
Outstretched in long, continuous blaze.
Before me all is hid from sight
By brooding mists, a moonless night,
Floods fathomless and infinite.
And now, how shall I find my way,
Shut from the light of cheerful day?
When storms arise and tempests blow,
Without a pilot must I go?
While raging passion's tempest brood
Raise hurricanes upon the flood,
Toss my frail vessel in the storm,
And mountain billows, high upborne,
Wash from life's blasted bark the helm,
And in their trough my decks o'erwhelm.
Lo, amongst rocky islands lost,
By contrary currents wildly tossed,
No helper near, no beacon guide,
Toward Destruction's rocks I ride;
And now e'en courage, trembling, quails;
Wrenched from the yards, the shattered sails
   Fly drifting with the wind;
Crash round the ship the billows roar,
Huge precipices lower before,
   A ragged coast behind.

Author of life! with veilèd face,
That from thine unseen dwelling-place
The track of destiny dost trace,
Grant, when I reach the boundless sea
Of unexplored eternity,
And join at last the ghostly train
Which ploughs that all unmeasured main,
That I to thee, with cheerful trust,
Commit my freight of cumbrous dust;
Yet when I cross that dismal sea,
Let me not unattended be;
Nor, when I bid farewell to land,
Ship with the passions' boisterous band;
Ill company such mutinous crew,
On unknown seas, when tempests brew.
Far different messmates would I know;
Let Truth and Justice with me go —
Justice to steer, while at the bow
Truth looks ahead with piercing sight,
Watching for breakers through the night.
And, Conscience, do thou there attend,
Parent of Truth, and Justice' friend;
Wide awake while others sleep,
Thou the compass safe must keep;
Still watchful, lest we veer too far
From the fixed light of Virtue's star;

And let mild Resignation go with me,
Of temper tranquil in the stormiest sea;
She, through the voyage so rough and long,
Shall lull the hours with plaintive song.
And, without fail, let Love be near,
Who hath of wind and wave no fear;
She, our physician, whose mild skill
Shall keep the crew all healthful still.

But, above all, let Hope be there;
She, 'midst the whirlpools of despair,
To thread each narrow channel knows;
She cares not for the whirlwind's shocks,
And safe o'er shoals and sunken rocks
Ploughs, singing as she goes.
Truth for our captain, and I'll trust the sea,
But let far-seeing Hope the pilot be;
With her for guide, all dangers shall be past;
With fearless skill she'll come to port at last,
And in heaven's azure wave her golden anchor
cast.

ODE TO OBLIVION.

O Night-descended, that, with sable wing,
Through the far past art veiling every thing!
How briefly, as thy mists roll onward, aught
Shines through their depths, or work of hands or
thought!
As clouds that cast afar their shadows gray,
And sweep the sunbeams from the hills away,
So truth thou veilest, light grows dark in thee,
And History hides in thine obscurity.
All things melt in thee; an unnumbered host
Time urges on, till all in thee are lost;
His children dear, the days, the months, the years,
Thou dost o'erwhelm, heedless of prayers and
tears;
Each in thy silent realm in darkness disappears.

Fame, Strength, Power, Beauty, in thine eyes are
nought;
Worthless all works that Genius' hand hath
wrought.
Lo, where yon once proud temples crumbling stand,
In ruined beauty smiling o'er the land,
Whose mouldering shafts, with green vines gayly
decked,

Even yet amaze; tottering, but still erect;
While fragment poised on fragment, high in air,
The grass-crowned capitals can scarcely bear;
Soon hurled to ruin all in dust must lie,
And lastly, Nature's self, like Art, must die.
There's nothing but is destined to decay;
Time, thine old servant, forced by thee to obey,
Mows with reluctant scythe all his own works
away.

Yet spare a while yon stone, and flowery bed,
Where Love, with anxious hand, adorns the dead;
And spare yon obelisk, o'ergrown with weeds,
Which tells the inspiring tale of virtuous deeds;
And save yon vine-clad oak from wintry blast,
Sacred so oft to friendship in the past;
Whose whispering boughs oft sighed to song and
tale,
Ere at Death's touch the tuneful lips grew pale.
Seize first those towers, that, raised in air sublime,
Tell of a long antiquity of crime.
O, vain to arrest thee, since thy power unbounded
All undermines, however firmly founded;
All in one common wreck must be confounded.

Yet from thy boundless charnel house, once more
Time shall his buried Beautiful restore.

Thou also hast a master; pitying Fate
Permits thee not all good to annihilate;
The just man's fame some fragrance leaves behind,
That with each age grows sweeter to mankind,
And from the seeds of loveliness, the earth,
Year after year, new beauty brings to birth;
The rough rocks into temples rise once more;
Men build their fanes more stately than before.
Thou canst consume but Beauty's grosser part;
But all that is most excellent in art
Survives thy power unharmed, deep in the human heart.

In vain, great enemy! dost thou employ
Thy might to undermine and to destroy;
Truth says, he vainly works who seeks to spoil;
Her sacred law at last shall thwart thy toil.
Even in long-buried ashes man can trace
The lines that teach the history of his race;
Old Egypt's records thou hadst hid in caves —
The tale is whispered from the mummies' graves;
Thy lavas turned vast cities to a tomb —
Earth cannot keep the secret in her womb;
Not even thy hottest fires have proved so strong,
But Science' eye, the cindered scrolls among,[28]
Reads plainly out once more the poet's idlest song.

Nature still more defies thee, where the past
Heaves forth its rifted wreck of reptiles vast,
Huge elephants, and many a beastly shape,
Whose bones thy slow-consuming grasp escape,
But shows no sign of intellectual man, —
Life most ignoble where life first began,
And Reason latest born; hence men may see
Foreshadowed a more bright futurity;
The world's great Builder doth His work restore
In every age more perfect than before;
Till life at last shall quite forget its tears,
More beauteous forms shall move through wider
 spheres,
Drawing nearer and more near to God through
 endless years.

Out then, poor child of Discord! since God's
 thought
Hath reasons for each work His hand hath
 wrought.
And shall I fear His wisdom is perplexed,
Since of His acts I cannot learn the next?
He made all for some end — His love divine
Knows best for what; it is no care of mine.
Enough, I'll trust, and laugh at thee, whose
 power,
O universal foe! must have its hour,

And cease. How weak, whom mortals deem so
strong!
Awhile thou shalt o'erwhelm, yet nothing long;
Thy work began ten million years ago,
But earth more fair with every age doth grow;
Scarce canst thou sweep yon frail bridge from
the sky,
Upon whose arch 'tis writ, life shall not die,
But God, in storm clouds veiled, rebuilds it in
the sky.

THE SPRING MORNING OF A BE-REAVED MAN.

Merry swallow, that wast twittering half the night
beneath my eaves,
And art thou come again, old friend, to greet the
opening leaves!
How gladly would I welcome thee, sweet harbinger
of spring,
That tellest me, my garden flowers again are blos-
soming.
Last year thy song delighted, it is nothing to me
now,

My flowers are out of mind, and no welcome guest
art thou,
For all things now seem saddest, that were sweetest to me then;
Fair swallow, fly away and seek the roofs of happier men;
Let friends that ne'er were parted, let the joyous
welcome thee;
O fly away, fly quickly, with thy chattering company.

The morning breeze blows freshly, bearing music
on its wing;
But the voice is hushed to silence, that was wont
for me to sing.
The fountains are all gushing, just filled with
showers of rain;
But the spring my life that comforted will never
flow again.
My flower that blossomed all the year, last winter
dropped away,
And withers now within the grave; O why art
thou so gay?
The hand that hath caressed thee, that hath fed
thee o'er and o'er,
Lies stiff and cold beneath the mould; thy mistress comes no more.

She loved thee too, and hadst thou died, she would
have wept for thee;
Then why dost thou, so thoughtless now, chirrup
thus merrily?

The summer shall come back again, the valleys
shall grow green,
And the vine shall stoop and lowly droop to min-
gle with the stream.
The oriole in the branching elm shall waken me
from slumber,
And all the trees shall fill the breeze with voices
without number;
And from his bed all rosy red, the sun shall rise at
morn,
And as of old shall paint with gold our field of
waving corn.
And when above in shady grove the plaintive wood,
thrush sings,
O'er lawn and lake his voice shall wake a host of
happy things.
But what delight in sound or sight can nature have
for me,
To whom the very grasshopper a burden seems
to be.

Then, lost one, when red twilight melts to the dull gray of eve,
The whippoorwill shall wail again, and seem for thee to grieve;
Thy mournful shade will come, sweet maid, with the declining light,
And the ticking clock thy step will mock through all the lonesome night.
Thy voice will whisper in the breeze, will murmur in the rain;
Earth will seem full of thee, but thou wilt never come again.
The sun so bright, the stars at night, a mournful look must wear,
For every grace in Natrue's face, grows loveless to despair.
Great God of love! thy world above would seem less fair to be,
Save that the dear can with us here in union worship thee.

But the green will grow to gray again, when autumn hath come back,
And the chestnut sheds in prickly beds its burs upon my track.

Then birds that lately were so blithe, shall cry with mournful sound,
While falling leaves in every breeze fly whirling round and round,
And the waterfowl in clouds shall howl, slow trailing through the sky,
While warblers light in gusty flight to warmer regions fly.
O, gladly would I join their train in foreign lands to roam,
And amongst thoughtless things forget the solitude of home.
They shall sing the songs of summer, they shall prate on every tree,
While I, in the lone greenwood, must ponder silently.

And grove and wood as red as blood shall next October glow,
When morning bright shall chase the night through mists as white as snow;
When the wain comes creaking through the field, and ripe fruits have grown mellow,
And the maples flout their boughs about in crimson and in yellow,
And red oaks, mingling with the mists that all the mountains crown,

Shall change their hue of vapory blue to a deep
russet brown;
When the sumach on the hillside glows like a
flaming cloud,
And the mill-wheel plies merrily, and the cataract
grows loud.
Fair forests! once in happier days how sweet ye
seemed when sere!
Ye mind me now of vanished joys;—ah, why
were ye so dear?

And the merry trout shall sport about within our
favorite brook,
Where oft we sat on leafy mat, to ponder o'er our
book;
While the partridge roamed the forest, and the
squirrel chattered shrill,
And over head the boughs hung dead, and all the
winds were still;
When the flowerless clematis grown old, had gained
a bristly beard,
And the crow screamed loud, from leafy shroud of
the dark pine groves heard;
When, hushed around, all other sound is silent as
the grave,
And asters blue shall mock the hue that gleams
beneath the wave.

All I shall see that gladdened me, except one well-known face;
When autumn weaves our couch of leaves, thy seat is empty space.

I shall tread back the well-known track, the book shall be forgot;
My feet shall pass through rustling grass to reach our lonely cot;
The light shall spill o'er every hill in showers of dazzling rays,
And from each sod the golden rod in every field shall blaze;
And katydid, through daylight hid, at eve his song shall sing,
And full of mirth before the hearth shall make the twilight ring;
While in the orchard the red owl mews from his apple tree,
And the grey one in the deep pine wood sits neighing mournfully;
To sound thy knell each voice shall swell, but thine no more I hear.
Fond friends! to dust return ye must, O why are ye so dear?

And when the boisterous winter winds around the
house shall howl,
And placed before thy empty seat is seen an
empty bowl,
When through the sky the clouds shall lie in one
broad sheet of gray,
And the keen blast to the dead past hath swept all
bloom away,
When in deep rest the river's breast lies cased in
glassy shield,
Ice far and wide on every side incrusting every
field,
When all around o'er trackless ground the drifted
snows are piled,
Through all the day no step to stray across the
pathless wild,
Until at last, light ebbing fast, Night's silent shad-
ows fall,
And spectres thin, through firelight dim, dance
flickering on the wall,

Then must I grieve through the long eve, and
spend the hours alone;
In gusts my ear shall seem to hear a fond, familiar
tone.
The poems we were wont to read I shall be musing
o'er,

But shut the book at those sad words, "Farewell,
we meet no more!"
And when grown old, December cold his dreariest
look shall wear,
And the merry chime of Christmas time comes
ringing through the air,
All round about, within, without, the carol, sound-
ing clear,
Shall seem to moan, "thou'rt all alone — a weary
wanderer here."
Thy voice through silent space will sound, thy
tread in every track;
Despair will ever call on thee, but thou wilt ne'er
come back.

At last, the spring o'er every thing shall sweetly
smile once more;
Her fragrant breath and winter's death shall Na-
ture's bloom restore;
And budding flowers, 'neath April showers, shall
wake from wintry sleep,
And the rustling vine aloft shall climb, and round
the windows creep.
Then the brown butterfly shall light on the last
bank of snow,[29]
And 'neath the shady pines the pale anemone shall
blow.

The tree, the flower, the bee, the bower, the sea-
fowl o'er the main,
The skies of blue, the squirrel too, shall all come
back again;
And then they say, the newborn May shall solace
bring to woe;
That growing years dry human tears, as Spring
drinks up the snow.

Why then, fair swallow, come again, if grief be
then grown old;
Yet foolish thing, what use to sing to one whose
heart is cold?
Can it delight, in sunshine bright, to see thee dive
and soar
Among my trees, when thou and these love's
raptures thrill no more?
Many there be will welcome thee, then let the song
be theirs;
Forbear thy strain, thou'lt soothe in vain a spirit
that despairs.
Farewell, and thanks to thee, yet sing no more be-
neath the eaves,
O wake me not, I'd sleep forgot, as sound as last
year's leaves;

I cannot bid thee welcome, merry harbinger of spring,
For a robe of woe my feelings throw round thee and every thing.

ROBERT BURNS.

A VISION OF HIS MAUSOLEUM AT DUMFRIES.

What marble dome salutes mine eyes,
Tipped with the pallid glow of eve?
They tell me here a poet lies,
Whose fate untimely bids me grieve.
Yet let me first thy history know,
Or ere I deign to mourn for thee;
Speak, shade of him that lies below!
For many kinds of bards there be;
Some, bravely free, have trod the earth like kings,
While some have cringed and crawled like grovelling things.

Didst thou with mercenary rhymes
Pander to power, or to thine age?
Or, silent at the oppressor's crimes,
Wast thou puffed up by patronage?

Did wrong from thee meet no reproof?
  Did merit rouse thy pride or spleen?
Would'st thou have gagged the mouth of truth
  With caustic wit or satire keen?
Then I'll not waste my time to read thy name;
Oblivion were for thee more fit than fame.

The more melodious were thy song,
  The less to hear should I have heart;
To the grand sum of human wrong
  Thou hast contributed thy part.
To wear the bays thou wast unfit;
  Thy brows had soiled the wreath divine;
At no pure shrine thy torch was lit;
  Sleep 'mongst the slighted wrecks of time.
Though sad thy tale, my heart no grief shall borrow;
Too well I know that guilt is sire of sorrow.

But didst thou lift or hand or voice
  T' uphold the right or aid the oppressed?
With woe didst weep, with joy rejoice?
  If kind affections warmed thy breast,
If thou hast sought to save from death
  The memory of neglected worth,
Or if thy muse, with honest breath,
  Called truth despised from darkness forth —
Whate'er thy faults, still will I honor thee,
So thou didst not desert sweet charity.

And though, in error's wilds benighted,
  The senses bound thee as their slave,
Till reason dimned, and memory blighted,
  Left thee in degradation's grave ;
Still be thy name to feeling dear,
  Still be thou pure in sight of heaven;
For thee let pity drop the tear;
  Thou hast loved much, and art forgiven.
Let no rude tongue disturb thy last repose,
Nor slight the debt mankind to genius owes.

Alas, poor bard! I know thee now;
  No mean, no hated name was thine ;
Yet though the bays were on thy brow,
  I feel thou wast but half divine.
Whom in my inmost heart I prize,
  From passion's thraldom must live free,
Himself must never need despise,
  Nor live even his own enemy ;
Must rather dwell unknown, from fame exempt,
Than sue to pity for her mild contempt.

Thou, too, had'st scarcely longed for fame,
  Had'st thou beheld their moistened eyes,
Who say, while here they read thy name,
  " The song was sweet, the man unwise."
O, child of genius, at what price
  Thou buildest upon empty sound!

Rather let cold oblivion's ice
  Congeal me nameless in the ground,
Than that ambition should prefer a tear,
To reverence mute, wrested from minds severe.

Speak, generous bard of Ayr, and say,
  Did those sweet lines with truth agree,[30]
Which said, Heaven's light could lead astray?
  Did heavenly light make wreck of thee?
Where, by old Dumfries' hallowed fane,
  Thy mouldering bones the cold sods press,
I hear thy warning voice exclaim,
  "The bane of genius is excess;
But who casts stones at me?" Ah, judgment halts,
And bids me love thee still with all thy faults,

Nor join that cold and heartless band,
  Who scorn thy sweet and simple rhymes,
And thank the Almighty that they stand
  Convicted but of lawful crimes.
They only steal the poor man's bread,
  Or lick the filthy feet of power,
Unhouse the friendless orphan's head,
  And rob the widow of her dower.
Yes, watchful Fame brings genius' faults to light,
While mean men's crimes oblivion hides in night.

TO A WORLDLING, TIRED OF COUNTRY LIFE.

O, WHO art thou, that 'mongst these trees
  Canst find for thought no calm retreat?
These boughs to thee are but "ship knees,"
  The grass mere hay beneath thy feet.

These mighty oaks, of shade immense,
  Thou reckonest at six crowns per ton;
Those hemlocks dost thou count in pence;
  All turns to gold thou lookest on.

O modern Midas! thou art one,
  Whose glance profanes these groves and streams,
To whose bleared eye yon golden sun
  But a gigantic dollar seems.

These fragrant flowers, that scent the air,
  These shady bowers, yield thee no pleasure;
And, from yon height, the landscape fair
  Only in acres canst thou measure.

To thee yon mountain seems a mine,
  Those greenwoods planks all straight and sound,
And the rich clusters of yon vine
  Hang, each a shilling in the pound.

Thou in these fertile fields dost stand,
And mourn the heaviness of time;
O fool! as if wise Nature's hand
E'er casts her priceless pearls to swine.

Like scum, thou mountest upward still,
To live with nature at topmast;
Buildest upon the highest hill,
To catch the sweep of every blast.

And when the autumn days draw nigh,
And woods their golden tints unfold,
Swift as the wild goose dost thou fly
To gloat on less unreal gold.

Thou grow'st more wretched day by day;
Much dost thou get, yet naught enjoy;
And when at last age makes thee gray,
Once more through dotage grown a boy,—

Thy schoolmaster is cankered care,
Thy learning, how life's joys to stint;
Thy sole resource against despair
Is to live cold and hard as flint.

Go, man of dross, and be less proud!
Be less the slave of spleen and pelf;

First learn, amidst the bustling crowd,
  To love thy neighbor like thyself.

Then come once more, these slopes ascend,
  Once more thy woodland walks renew ;
If thou art grown of man the friend,
  Then may'st thou dwell with nature too.

Oft from these hill-tops hast thou seen
  Her face all fresh with vernal glow ;
Come when the desolated scene
  Presents a boundless waste of snow.

If thou hast purified thy heart,
  These prospects shall no desert seem ;
Earth shall be fair in every part,
  And winters white as summers green.

Then shall thy soul, no more forlorn,
  Enjoy at last life's greatest boon,
When dark December's night of storm
  Seems kind as this sweet day in June.

Then, tranquilly thy trustful soul
  Shall float on fortune's restless sea,
Shall hear all round fate's thunders roll,
  Disaster's lightning flash shall see

Unmoved. King over self, 'mongst men
A mightier monarch shalt thou be;
For destiny shall govern them,
Whilst thou shalt govern destiny.

POET AND TOLL-GATHERER.

A CONVERSATION AT THE FOOT OF MOUNT PARNASSUS.

"Friend, ope thy gate and let me pass,
And what's to pay for climbing here?"
"Not much, one as; mind, not one ass,[31]
For that I trow would cost thee dear;
Were I so paid by each who passes,
I now were worth a million asses."

"Nay, nay! lead forth that horse, I pray,
Whose back all bards are wont to mount;
It is my wish to reach this day
The waters of that crystal fount,
Around whose brink the Muses nine
Are wont to sing their hymns divine."

"Now tell me, stranger, in what land,
Ne'er trod by traveller's foot, thou dwellest?

That in these days would'st seek the band
  Of those lost maids of whom thou tellest?
They, and the horse, for aught I know,
Were dead three thousand years ago.

But scarce an hundred thousand horses,
  Though saddled all through night and day,
Could carry the unnumbered forces
  That daily up this hill-side stray
To notch their names upon the stair
Of the old ruined Temple there."

" Good man, I too have come full far,
  To worship at Apollo's fane;
But not his sacred stones to mar
  By carving there my worthless name.
Yet now, I pray thee, briefly say
How I may mount the easiest way."

" If thou art rich, some brother drudge
  Will gladly stoop to be thy hack;
If poor, bear others, for I judge
  Thy brains will scarcely break thy back.
We hope to have a railroad soon,
Then calves may reach their native moon.

Ofttimes a dozen, halt or maimed,[32]
  Some of left legs, and some of right,

Go in a body closely chained,
And thus the journey grows more light;
For each, well dovetailed to his brothers,
With his one leg helps all the others

And he, who must have staid below,
If with one foot obliged to delve,
Though he be blind, thus safe may go,
And climb the rugged mount on twelve;
Still easier task, when from behind
Blown onward by opinion's wind.

Thou could'st join these." "Churl! curb thy speech,
Or I'll report thee to the god,
And tell him, when the top I reach,
His servant's back requires a rod."
"O would e'en now he might appear,
To stay this mob from mounting here!

All night, their gongs, and yells, and cries,
Keep me awake." "What! on this hill
No longer to the listening skies
Chant those fair maids when winds are still?
Tell me, and hath the offended god
In sorrow left his blest abode?"

"Thou'lt find him not." "Then who will teach?"
"Fear not, there, bores of every nation
Thou'lt meet; there, hear all Babel's speech.
Yet, friend, if bent on education,
Thou'lt find, in many a lonely nook,
Viol, and lute, and music book.

For on this god-abandoned hill
Are many mansions. Wise and weak
Here worship Phœbus' image still;
His followers many a language speak;
And each an instrument can find
Tuned to such airs as suit his mind.

Through pipes of clay, and trumps of tin,
The windy voice of some is sent;
Some try the cymbals' crashing din,
Or trombone, noisy instrument,
Which the stunned god long kept concealed,
Till lost Pompeii's wrecks revealed.[33]

Some, mellower-eared, aspire to sound
The flute, or oboe clear and thin;
Some the deep viol's tone profound,
Some the light wreathing violin;
While some attune the sacred rhyme
To the grand organ's voice sublime.

But most now herd with that new school,
  Which roams from sense and sound astray;
Whose rambling tunes, despising rule,
  Howl like some Chinese orchestra:
More harsh than angry cats that fright
The stillness of a summer's night.

Yet, while the sounds so different be,
  Still less in concord with each other
The thoughts and sentiments agree;
  Seldom, in bard, bard finds a brother.
'Twixt false and true such friendship grows
As holds 'twixt nightingales and crows.

There shalt thou find, in conclave joined,
  That class which Plato hath derided,[34]
Whose sense is from the sage purloined;
  There those, who, by no reason guided,
Are but as mouthpieces admired,
And bray, like Balaam's ass, inspired.

Still others mar the sacred hymn,
  With hateful words and fiendish clang;
Or, with harsh accents and loud din,
  Join doleful drawl to pious twang.
Their brains, in taste or sense unskilled,
By cramming, like a sausage, filled.

Here, some, absorbed in sensual dream,
  To Bacchus vow the hymn unblest;
This one invokes Love's fickle queen,
  And that, the Demon of unrest;
While few to master skill aspire,
Touched with the warmth of heavenly fire.

Such state of things, endured for long,
  The god beheld with silent pain.
Few sought his seat through love of song,
  While oft the vile, through lust of gain,
Scorning the sacred spring to taste,
Sought but to lay his temple waste.

They bore his sacred urns away;
  His shafts they break, his bays they lop;
Each senseless idler fain would say
  He'd bellowed from the mountain's top,
And, to reward his worthless toil,
Our priceless relics needs must spoil;

Until at last the god, grown tired,
  Went down to dwell in secret places.
And now in glens and groves retired,
  Afar from noise and brazen faces,
Roams where his harmonies allure
Few save the humble and the pure."

"How can this be, O ancient man?
  For we below are wont to hear
That the god bids all climb who can,
  And drink those waters fresh and clear.
Hath he not willed that all who mount
Shall grow inspired at his own fount?"

"Deem not Castalia's crystal tides,
  E'er yet, the gift of song inspired;
Thither the crafty serpent glides,
  Where once the thirsty god retired.
The soaring and the creeping thing,
Both stoop to drink at the same spring;

Both rise refreshed — the snake, to bite;
  The god, more fit for sacred duty;
One hastens straight to shun the light,
  The other seeks the world of beauty.
Each strengthened, or for good or ill,
Departs, what Nature made him still."

A VISION OF THE WESTERN WORLD.

WHERE, in the far and boundless west,
  The sire of waters proudly flows,
Bears the tall ship upon his breast,
  And scatters plenty as he goes; —

Where, 'twixt gray bluffs and valleys green,
  The raft glides like a floating town,
While steamers swift, with shrilly scream,
  In panting haste ply up and down; —

Where the palmetto lightly ploughs
  The sighing gale with fan-like leaf,
And the dark cypress' moss-grown boughs
  Droop o'er the turbid wave beneath; —

There once I stood when life was new,
  And gazed upon the boundless tide;
The earth was wet with evening dew;
  My gun lay idle at my side.

And through the shades that round me fell,
  The moon her silvery mantle cast;
And whippoorwill her tale 'gan tell
  To the swift current sweeping past.

When lo! advancing on the wave,
  A wondrous vision met my sight;
All mute and tranquil as the grave,
  It moved upon the waters bright.

A silvery mist the deep o'erspread,
  And, down the river moving slow,
A reverend and majestic head
  Leaned on a hand as white as snow.

The countenance was mildly grave,
  Like what the ancient sculptor wrought
Who life to that pale marble gave,[35]
  Where glows old Tiber's face of thought.

Serene and godlike was the brow;
  In drizzly flume his locks descended;
His beard, which did his breast o'erflow,
  In glittering icicles depended.

Struck at the sight with awe profound,
  My wondering eyes beheld entranced;
I kneeled with reverence on the ground,
  While slow the stately form advanced.

I watched his proud and lofty air,
  Scarce deemed such nobleness could be,

Transcending all things bright and fair,
  Such wonderful tranquillity.

Now I, though but an idle wight,
  Yet loved all excellence to see;
And though I toyed with trifles light,
  The beautiful was dear to me.

But yet, although to manhood grown,
  My troubled spirit knew no rest;
No guiding law my thoughts had known,
  And aimless longings filled my breast.

Bereft of hope, I careless roved,
  And every formless phantom chased;
Onward a dreaming ghost I moved;
  The world seemed but a tangled waste.

" O, give me, Heaven," I oft would say,
  " Some sacred truth to feel and know,
That I might follow night and day,
  Till life should like these waters flow."

So, when I saw that spirit's face,
  All beaming with the inward mind;
Gladly would I have run his race,
  And all earth's cares have left behind.

The spirit read my inmost thought,
  And on the waters rested still;
These words the breezes whispering brought:
  " Thou hast the wish, but lackest will.

" Born in the mountain's lap was I,
  Far in the cold and gloomy north,
Where drifted snows unmelting lie,
  And restless winds go howling forth; —

" Where sun-gilt cliffs, grey, steep, and tall,
  Stand frowning o'er the torrent's foam,
Where, by the deafening waterfall,
  The bravest hunter fears to roam.

" From the dark cavern's deep recess
  I issued first a babbling rill,
Well pleased my onward course to press,
  And gaily plunge o'er height and hill.

" Sometimes compressed in narrow glen,
  My angry waves would boil and hiss;
But soon I'd break my bounds, and then
  Leap laughing down the deep abyss.

" Sometimes I flowed through forests green,
  Where earth her loneliest aspect wears,

And nought disturbs the silent scene
  Save haggard wolves and grizzly bears.

" Sometimes, walled up in basin wide,
  My restless steps ran round and round,
Then would I burst the mountain's side,
  And headlong dash to depths profound.

" At last the busy hand of man
  Would stay my course or fix my bound;
Swift would I break the obstructing dam,
  And scatter desolation round.

" The ruined village there behold,
  The tottering spire, the uprooted tree;
The shepherd vainly seeks his fold;
  The husbandman no crop shall see.

" Long since grown tame, my noiseless wave
  Disdains to scatter waste and woe.
I seek not to destroy, but save,
  Dispensing blessings as I go.

" For I, with life, have gathered strength,
  And strength should scorn the weak to oppress ;
My foes all vanquished now, at length
  I seek to fertilize and bless.

"No longer violent and wild,
My course is straight, and calm, and still;
The man hath put away the child;
I carve the valley at my will.

"Within my bosom deep and wide,
My power protects each entering rill;
Its work I teach, each movement guide,
That all their duty may fulfil.

"Swift o'er my breast the steamer glides;
Joyous the snowy sail expands;
I bear the ship to ocean's tides,
And urge her on to distant lands.

"So do I live from day to day,
Nor think how long my task may be;
Working for good through all my way.
Farewell; I seek my destiny."

"Spirit," I cried, "one moment stay!
O, tell me, whither dost thou tend?
Answer, if thou hast power to say,
Where will thy life's long labors end?"

"Ask him," said he, "who bade me wend
My way unquestioned to the sea.

With the broad ocean soon I blend,
  There wait what work remains for me.

"Perhaps in clouds and mist my form
  Shall from the ocean's breast exhale,
And o'er those peaks where I was born
  Again descend in storm and gale.

"Perhaps, absorbed within the sea,
  My restless waves shall cease to roll,
And, mingling with immensity,
  Blend formless in the unbounded whole.

"Ask me not how, nor when, nor where;
  Still to flow on is my behest;
Duty — 'tis but for that I care;
  To the world's God I leave the rest."

Fain had I spoke once more, but he
  Had vanished on the floods away;
Nought but the moonlight could I see,
  That gleamed upon the glittering spray.

Full long I viewed the waves afar,
  Till, fain to seek my grassy bed,
I woke; there was nor moon nor star;
  The sun was risen an hour o'erhead.

A CHAT WITH THE MEDICEAN VENUS.

" WHENCE art thou, maiden, that, with fixéd gaze,
  Dreadest intruding foot? Feel thou no fear;
One, only to admire thee, hither strays;
  No ruffian comes — there is no tempter near."

" Ah, sir, full many an age a maid I stand,
  Nor yet grow old. I am as life in death,
And wait here at Cleomenes' command,
  Who gave existence, but forgot my breath.

" Deep in the solid rock my limbs were bound,
  Till that deliverer came to set me free;
At last my prison cell his chisel found,
  And gladly I sprang forth to liberty.

" Alas, good man! he labored many a day
  My glossy limbs their gracefulness to teach;
But Pluto snatched him from this earth away,
  Just as my lips he would have formed for speech.

" So to thy mind mine eyes must dart my thought,
  Since by my tongue to express them I'm not free;
Full many an age his countenance I've sought,
  But all in vain. Good stranger, should you see,

Ask for my tongue." "Nay, now, excuse, for know,
Thy chiefest charm I in thy silence see;
Speech had dispersed thy lovers long ago;
Full half the world have cause to envy thee.

"Rejoice then in thy silence, and excuse
Thine author, since one greater lack remains:
The man was wise, who did a tongue refuse,
Where he had been so niggardly of brains."[36]

ODE TO HOPE.

Daughter of Joy! if she, who grasped thy wings,
Lest thou to Heaven shouldst 'scape from that dark den,
Whence sped o'er earth such hosts of hateful things,
No other service may have done for men,—
Still were it right that frail Pandora's name
Should be immortal on the rolls of Fame,
Since her blest gift to man all others puts to shame.

And, if my mind the unjust decree of Fate
Condemn, that caged a spirit born to aspire,

And doomed thee long to herd, in loathsome state,
With sin and sorrow, may it more admire
That worth, whose loss filled those sad sprites with dread;
Hell was half happy, till it deemed thee dead,
Nor wholly hateful grew, till thou for aye had'st fled.

O, cheerful spirit, that canst spotless live
In the same house with Evil! hating not,
Pitying whom Charity can scarce forgive,
And cheering those thy sisters had forgot;
Thou, in the worst, some germs of good wilt see,
And still, with sighs, all these remember thee,
And love, even while they scorn both Faith and Charity.

Yet now, ah me! the gift I half despise;
Thy speech so fair, yet ever filled with lies;
Why dost thou promise good, but ne'er fulfil?
Thou soothest, cheerest, yet deceivest still.

See, through the world, toward thee what lengthening train
Of wearied wretches turn their wistful eyes;
Where Freedom falls, and Justice pleads in vain;
Where blue-eyed Peace from armed Oppression flies,

And Truth, though chained, still calm, in Error's
dungeon lies.
I see her friendless, yet with stately air,
Stern-faced and proud, disdaining to despair;
Lo, through her grate, across the trackless waste,
She views thee, and forgets the guilty past,
Deeming, in Death's long sleep, her foe shall rest
at last.

I also knew thee, in those years
When the young hours, in smiles and tears,
Strolled slowly on; but since, at last,
With swifter feet they hurry past,
With faces grave, and eyelids dry,
No longer moved to smile or sigh,
More and more rarely comest thou;
Dim grows the wreath that crowns thy brow,
And scarce I dare to seek thee now;
Since, wont companionless to rove
In the deep shadows of that grove,
Where bearded Science spends his age,
Absorbed in book, or pictured page,
Or armed with microscope, to note,
Those tiny living swarms that float
Within the compass of a tear,
Or count those nations that appear
Beneath the surface of that main,

Whose tides flow in a drop of rain;
Living whole ages in an hour,
Hung from the petals of a flower,
Where the light wings of summer shower
Have cast their globe to shine and die,
When the first sunbeam bursts the sky.

Or, with that greater glass, when I survey
Those glittering orbs that swim through night and day
In endless space; to whom our distant sphere
Seems scarcely larger than a trickling tear,
Alas, the world seems grown so vast,
And man so mean, that now, at last,
Thou seemest fled to some far shore;
I must gaze after thee no more.
Yet, midst my night, I feel thy wavy wing,
And seem to hear thy sweet voice whispering,
"Even in that little drop I am,
Cheering the atom as the man."
Yes, in all life, I feel thou art,
Beating throughout all Nature's heart;
In sun, and moon, and twinkling star,
And every planet, near or far,
Even in this drop of vinegar,
That teems with life, I scarce can doubt
The pygmies there have found thee out;
Boasting, with all the vanity of men,

That the whole universe was made for them;
Each deeming his own world God's only sphere;
Each with some faith perhaps which he holds
dear;
While priests, inspired by thee to teach,
Go forth to proselyte and preach,
And the decaying faith renew,
All in a tiny drop of dew.
Who knows? not I,—yet, in my sight,
They wheel and whirl in such delight,
That howe'er trifling be their care,
Almost I deem thou must be there;
And since all Nature joys in thee,
I also of thy train would be.

O come, with heaven-born Trust, and scare
From earth the Demons of Despair;
Doubt, that hath lost all faith in Good;
Despondency, that loves to brood,
A gloomy monster, that begat
Pale Fear; and he, that other brat,
Suspicion, foe to Love and thee.
And when all these from earth shall flee,
Do thou and Charity, once more,
Her golden crown to Peace restore.
Not Chaos' child, but Truth's, on earth unknown
of yore,

When oft through lack of joy,
Men would themselves destroy;
And, wanting thee, oft fled to strife,
Doomed to a brief and brutish life.

Again from heaven descend,
A fond, a faithful friend,
And tame those restless passions, which, in vain,
The unaided power of Virtue can restrain.
Descend, a spirit fair and bright,
Outstretch, o'er all the earth, thy wings of light,
And chase away for aye the darkness of our night.

For thou canst soothe the weary hours
Of all who climb Life's rugged hill;
Canst strew its downward path with flowers;
Then cease not to deceive us still.

When first the new-waked Sun to birth
Emerged from chaos dark and wild,
Thy features charmed the infant Earth;
On thee the face of Nature smiled.

Thy visions cheer the enraptured eyes
Of Hermit lone in desert den;
Inspired by thee, he can despise
The frowns of Fate, the smiles of men.

Toward thee, from self-inflicted pain,
  Yon fast-worn Fakir lifts his eyes;
The Pilgrim, sinking on the plain,
  To thee looks up and joyful dies.

Thou canst the Sailor's fears assuage;
  Through thee, while sinking in the wave,
He can defy the tempest's rage,
  And smile within his wat'ry grave.

Thou, in the Soldier's battle hour,
  When Death most pitiless appears,
Canst make him brave the fiery shower,
  And yield his breath with shouts and cheers.

Thou even the grave with flowers canst deck,
  And warm the depths of Earth's cold womb,
When smiling over Nature's wreck,
  Thou sittest singing on the tomb.

Since first, the new created bow
Thy hand o'er heaven's blue arch didst throw,
  Men's tongues have hymned thy praise.
There, smiling upon Nature's birth,
Thou gavest the rejoicing Earth,
  Promise of happier days.

Come then, unload this weight of care,
And, from the deep caves of Despair,
O lift my spirit up;
And in thy gayest dress appear,
And quick, my fainting soul to cheer,
Present thy nectared cup.

Be present, too, in dying hour,
For thou alone, sweet Hope, hast power
To cheer the parting breath;
To make the enshackled Soul smile to be free,
Rend from the pitiless Grave his victory,
And steal the sting from Death.

ODE TO FANCY.

FAREWELL, Enchantress! Reason hath forbid
Me in thy temples more to bend the knee;
Until, at last, thy countenance is hid,
And, if I sought, thou scarce wouldst smile on me.
Thy reign is past.
Thy fires are quenched; thy golden dreams are o'er;
The days of rapture must return no more,
Too bright to last.

No gorgeous landscapes as of old appear,
  Seen through thy oriels, warm with rosy stain.
The light, that guides me now, is coldly clear;
  Thy glorious visions come not back again;
    Their tints decay.
Thy painted windows Truth hath oped so wide,
That the gay colors melt on every side
    To leaden gray.

My castles, built in air, are vanishing;
  The spirit voices of the evening cease;
The sphery music will no longer ring;
  Yon bow hath broke its covenant of peace,
    Though radiant still.
The bond 'twixt man and the immortal powers
Seems but the transient work of sportive showers
    That sweep the hill.

Thine eye, averted now, no more from far
Will read my fortune in some twinkling star;
No naiad sports upon the flood,
The elves are banished from the wood,
No mermaids sing in coral caves,
No sea-god rides upon the waves,
And nymphs, that guarded grove and rill,
And dwarfs, that peopled every hill,
And knights of fairy land, and ladies gay;—

All fled, the enchanted gardens fade away,
And only leave behind sad relics of decay.

And yet, why should I mourn, joy of my youth,
That thou hast found an enemy in Truth!
Thine uncurbed brood, through ages drear and blind,
Have ruled as ruthless tyrants o'er mankind.
Ah, happy, when no more misled by thee,
Men shall forget their feuds and cruelty.
Truth from the earth hath purged the darker crimes
Caused by thy wild caprice in former times.
The age of feudal servitude is past;
No guiltless wretches to the flames are cast;
Wizard and witch with thy false lights have vanished;
And, when her patron, Ignorance, shall be banished,
Shall Superstition from her throne be hurled,
Thy bastard child, who long hath ruled the world;
She, of thy base-born progeny the last.
Then coward Fear shall fly, and Error's reign be past.

And, when those baleful sprites are fled,
And, like one risen from the dead,
Love, without rod, shall rule mankind,
And all in brotherhood shall bind;

When ancient evil is forgot,
And guilt, and grief, remembered not,
And godlike Reason peoples earth
With beings of diviner birth;
Why then, sweet Fancy, come once more,
Not crowned a Monarch, as of yore,
But, on grave Wisdom's steps attend,
Rather as servant than as friend,
Contented at his feet to sit,
And with thy brethren, Mirth and Wit,
Sometimes to drown with jest and tale
The growling storm or whistling gale.

Then to thine ancient temples come again,
Thine altars bright with no unhallowed flame,
The Virtues by thy side; and at the feast
Stand thou a courteous host, no more high-priest;
And, dressed in robes of purest white,
That cast a lustre on the night,
Wait, leaning on the arm of sacred Truth,
To inspire once more the glorious dreams of youth.
But let thine ornaments allure
Neither to acts nor thoughts impure;
But through the broad, well builded hall,
Adorn each niche and pedestal
With busts of many a saint and sage,
The glory of a by-gone age,
Becrowned with flowers and garlands gay,

Plucked freshly from the lap of May;
And paint the walls and windows o'er
More brightly than thou didst of yore;
Nor only let thy pictures please the eye,
But charm the soul, and lift it to the sky.
Alas, if thou with Virtue must be friended,
Ere with mankind, thy days on earth are ended!
Then fly not yet, nor cease to smile,
But fold thy wings and wait awhile,
Lest Reason, robbed of thee, seem too severe;
Lest Love grow cold when thou no more art near;
And life a dreary void, without a smile or tear.

Steal on yon wight in furry robe,
Whose eyes are fixed on map and globe;
And kindle up his twilight gray
With light that never leads astray;
Intrude not, decked with gaudy hue
Of purple, crimson, green and blue;
But, with a lustre pale and mild,
Illume his cell for Science' child.
Come smiling, clad in mellowest light
Of sunny gold or silvery white;
There sport amidst the rays that fall
Through stained glass of cloistered hall,
Where, 'neath the dusty, glimmering beams,
That slanting float in hazy streams,
Built round with books, the hoary sage

Sits poring o'er his musty page,
Shut in some antique hermitage.

Nor less cheer yon poor wretch, whose unschooled
thought
By Art or Science' tongue was never taught;
Who tired and worn with ceaseless toil,
No longer ploughs the fallow soil,
But, by the chimney corner sits,
And sleeps, and wakes, and sighs by fits.
Come to that lonely one, in gay attire,
Sweeten his cup, enliven his dull fire,
Teach him how, loosed from inward strife,
He may spin out the hours of life
To a long autumn of content,
Till Death, on fatal errand sent,
Shall deem Fate hath misread the time,
And, loath to spoil so green a vine,
E'en turn his back upon the door,
Resolved to wait some ten years more.

Visit the prisoners, who in dungeon damp
Pine ceaseless; trim for these Hope's dying lamp;
Soothe yon sad son of trade, who longs to flee
From eating cares, and lean anxiety;
Cheer the desponding; warn the too elate,
Since poor and rich, the humble and the great,

Need thee alike; nay, even the wise, forsooth!
Who scorns to fear, needs other friend than Truth,
Would he enjoy in age the cheerful glow of youth.

I, too, if in this vale of tears
I should wear out my fourscore years,
At last may thank thee for thine aid.
Not now, O come not yet, fair maid!
But when I shall grow weak and old,
And in my veins the blood runs cold,
And long secluded from delight,
I shall have learned to read aright
In Wisdom's book; become so wise,
That marvels can no more surprise,
Still following Truth in all her range,
Till nought in Nature shall seem strange;—
Then, Fancy, once again I'll woo thee,
More warmly that I need not rue thee,
Since I, in Learning's cause grown gray,
No more shall fear to go astray.
Whilst thou, in sage Experience' school,
Shalt have forgot to play the fool,
And, haply tamed by thought and years,
Shalt have outlived the age of tears;
Firm friends once more, I, in thy once loved bowers
Again will pluck the long neglected flowers,
And with thy sparkling cup, cheer worn out Life's
last hours.

THE POET.

FIRST TREATMENT.

THE LOVE OF ART REWARDS THE PURSUIT OF IT.

Guest of the gods! men say thy lot
  Was ever hard and friendless found;
Doomed on that earth to dwell forgot,
  Which thou hast made all hallowed ground—
As if the debt men owe thy strains,
  In gold or praises can be paid!
Thy music falls like freshening rains,
  Or sunlight in the forest shade.
He hath enough, who holds a gift so high,
The good to cheer, the bad to purify.

The lyre is in itself a treasure
  Of priceless value to the bard;
The artist's skill his wealth must measure;
  The song must be its own reward.
They little know what joys are thine
  That live for vanity's display;
Opinion makes their wealth, while thine
  Man cannot give nor take away.

Even kings themselves have begged a song of thee,
To soothe the sense of the soul's poverty.

What though the scorn of senseless pride
  Disdain thy poor and humble lot?
Though fools thy sacred songs deride —
  Nay, though by all mankind forgot?
Yon tuneful thrush no witness wants,
  When his wild carols charm the glade;
If steps profane invade his haunts,
  He wings his way to deeper shade,
Where, all unseen, within the gloomy wood,
His plaintive song delights the savage solitude.

THE POET.

SECOND TREATMENT.

A REPROOF OF MELANCHOLY.

O THOU, that know'st with stately strain
  To soothe the restless hours of care;
Why waste thy skill in moanings vain?
  Why wake the accents of despair?
The cheerful lyre was lent thee but to bless;
Why add new pangs to human wretchedness?

Yet had the bard this calling only,
  To make dull days more dark appear,
And cheerless solitudes more lonely,
  And dreary prospects doubly drear,
I'd fly the Muses, and their dark-draped halls,
For blithe Silenus and his bacchanals.

Since time is brief, let man enjoy;
  The wise disdain the sullen mood.
Waits Evil, watching to destroy?
  Let us o'ercome him, then, with good,
And leave the bad to frown through life's fair day,
Or waste in moping the swift hours away.

Ope not thy lips, sad child of song;
  I know what answer thou wilt make;
Thou'lt say, the sight of ceaseless wrong
  Bids thee lament for others' sake,
Because, the wide world through, thine eyes can see
No spot unsoiled by crime and misery;

That in the strife for wealth and power,
  The worst must still triumphant be;
That Virtue lives so brief an hour,
  While Guilt a lengthened date doth see.
Sad fool! forbear thy melancholy rhyme;
Good cannot find an enemy in Time,

Who hath no temper of his own,
But from our thoughts each mood derives.
Be sure all reap as they have sown,
In fruits of good or evil lives;
And he, who most hath thwarted Nature's plan,
Is oftenest still the disappointed man.

Virtue can make misfortune gay,
And Love, the load of sorrow light;
And with these two Hope loves to stay,
Him cheering, who keeps these in sight.
'Tis true each morrow dawns on scenes untried;
But the wise mind will view the brightest side.

Yet if thy wayward, restless soul
Would still the war with wisdom wage,
Spurn sickly Fancy's weak control,
Be less of bard, and more of sage.
Live just and free, and though thy path be rough,
Be of good cheer; to be a man's enough.

Though song's sad children pass away,
Time can their wasted ranks renew;
But Nature's self must feel decay,
When stern and vigorous wills grow few.
Truth vainly speaks in sweet, prophetic numbers,
When courage fails and godlike reason slumbers.

Great gods! when ye your gifts reclaim,
  May I with cheerfulness resign
The world of sense, but still retain
  Unsullied Truth and Love divine;
The pencil's charm, the chisel's marble birth,
Hide in the bowels of a frozen earth.

Melt poesy in air away,
  Let music to the tempests fly;
Let Nature's every charm decay,
  And in eternal winter lie;
But leave these two, and courage to live free,
That human life lose not its poetry.

Then, though each muse have hid her face,
  The rosy hours, the days, the years,
With a new joy shall run their race;
  Grief shall almost forget her tears;
And Truth, and Love, and Liberty divine,
When the last Poet's runes have ceased to chime,
With sweeter strains shall smooth the wrinkled
    brow of Time.

THE POET.

THIRD TREATMENT.

WHEREIN HE BOASTS HIS DESTINY.

O THOU, with brows as black as night,
  That hurryest 'mongst the busy throng!
Whose ear no music can delight,
  Still following mammon all day long,

Seeking for comfort out of care,
  Thou still on sorrow's path dost press,
Thinking to drive away despair
  By an industrious idleness.

O son of strife! will all this broil
  The joys or hours of life prolong?
Thou canst not reach, with all thy toil,
  The raptures of my idlest song.

Born on misfortune's barren wild,
  I'm happy, though my path be rough;
When Phœbus, on his favorite child,
  Bestowed the lyre, he gave enough.

In me doth childhood's heart delight,
While Age forgets his slow decay;
I nerve the soldier's arm in fight,
I bless the pilgrim on his way.

When fierce Oppression's hated brood
The ages chain in hopeless night,
Till man, at last, despairs of good,
And scarcely dares to dream of light;

My voice can pierce the gloom profound,
And with new hope fill every heart;
The trump of Liberty I sound,
And make the affrighted tyrant start.

I melt the soul at Pity's tale,
Make man his selfishness forget.
Where'er Affliction makes her wail,
Or earth with human tears is wet,

Swift as the wind, lo! there am I;
And while my strings their strains prolong,
Pale Care, entranced, forgets to sigh,
And Sorrow's voice is drowned in song.

And when at last I yield my breath,
I still shall live in glorious rhyme;

And, through the gloomy gates of death,
  Sail singing down the stream of time.

Great Jove hath named me child of Heaven,
  And bid me pass his portals free;
And Fate hath to the poet given
  A twofold immortality.

For while with gods his spirit lives,
  Men's tongues shall his loved strains prolong;
Thus in two spheres the bard survives,
  Deathless alike in soul and song.

THE POET.

FOURTH TREATMENT.

A RECEIPT FOR MAKING ONE.

And would'st thou join the immortal band
  That wake the lyre with master skill?
Yet many a bard, though bold of hand,
  And light of touch, and firm of will,
Hath failed to urge the magic strings
Beyond the clink of tinkling things.

Then first, ere thou begin, be sure
   That on thy hopes the muses smile?
For if thy love of song be pure,
   Though thou wert wrecked on desert isle,
The tuneful shell would charm thine ear,
When none but savage beasts could hear.

And learn with reverent love to prize
   The lyre that Heaven hath briefly lent;
He who to highest skill would rise,
   Must not despise his instrument;
Hence perfect grew the immortal choirs,
Whom love of their own art inspires.

Next be upright; for though thy hand
   Great Phœbus' self should stoop to train,
No excellence canst thou command,
   Dost thou the simple truth disdain;
But thou shalt yield to him whose thought
By plain sincerity was taught.

For to the false, the vain, the weak,
   The gods' own lyre yields no sweet voice;
Not genius' self can make it speak,
   Save with a wild, discordant noise,
Till the musician's soul shall be
Tuned with his harp in harmony.

Next Science seek, though fools deride,
  For she to truth must lead the way;
And never roam from Reason's side,
  Lest Fancy tempt thy steps astray;
But let thy wit be well content
To serve as wisdom's ornament.

Let not Prosperity seduce;
  Receive her as a formal guest;
And to Adversity's abuse
  Present a spirit undepressed;
And ever live from brawls exempt;
Hold rank and riches in contempt.

Live free, and strive to make men so,
  Though driven to dwell with nations rude.
No flowers of poesy can grow
  On the bleak wastes of servitude.
Learn to disdain all worthless things,
And flatter neither mobs nor kings.

Love beauty, which is truth to love:
  These of perfection parents are.
Yet must thou soar gross sense above,
  Whilst charmed with all things good and fair.
Thy temper restless must aspire,
Yet rule a monarch o'er desire.

Revere the All-Wise, but feel no fear;
  Serve neither creed, nor clique, nor place.
But live half jovial, half austere,
  Teacher and friend of all thy race;
So mingling tenderness with truth,
That both may love thee, Age and Youth.

And learn betimes in nature's face
  Each nicer feature to descry,
Each transient character to trace;
  Hold fellowship with cloud and sky,
With bird, and beast, and flower, and tree,
The running brook, and roaring sea.

And oft in solitude to wander,
  And oft in watches of the night
Upon God's works and laws to ponder,
  Till Silence' self shall yield delight,
Retire betimes; yet in such mood
As feels in all that each is good.

Until at last, grown old and wise,
  Thy skill such solace shall impart,
That thou in prophecy shalt rise
  Above the fame of Orpheus' art.
He feeling taught to rock and tree;
But they shall gain a tongue from thee.

Methinks thou sayest, "Restrain thy speech;
The bard was ever but a fool.
Thy dull philosophy go teach
To them that throng the sages' school."
If such thy thought, my task is done;
For sage and perfect bard are one.

But if the spirit pricks thee still,
And to go farther thou hast heart,
Then add to Wisdom's higher skill
The special secrets of thine art;
For without these an angel's speech
Must fail the loftiest strains to reach.

Teach the truth clearly; not like them
That wrap the thought in wordy cloud;
Fear rather lest the wise condemn,
Than court the clamors of the crowd.
That he who runs can read thy sense,
Deem thou thy greatest excellence.

Yet think not truth, or sense alone,
Will satisfy the tasteful mind;
The varying notes with truthful tone
Must in rich harmony be joined,
Till in such lofty strains they roll,
As charm the ear, and chain the soul.

Thy skill must blend the sense and sound
  In a sweet concord, chaste, severe,
Till poesy from earthly ground
  Mounts to a more celestial sphere,
And less like mortal language seems,
Than music from the land of dreams.

Yet while thou soar'st in heaven afar,
  Thy brethren thou must ne'er forget;
But backward to thy native star
  Must look with fond affection yet.
Be this the climax of thine art,
To teach the mind, yet touch the heart.

For all delights of soul or sense,
  All good that wealth or power commands,
All forms of glorious excellence,
  Moulded by thought or made with hands,
On earth beneath — in heaven above,
All are as nothing without love.

THE RIVER REVISITED.

OR, LIFE'S EXPERIENCE.

THE clouds have capped the mountain's brow;
 The stream runs darkly clear below;
So rested they, so flowedst thou,
 Sweet river, twenty years ago.

When standing on thy flowery bank,
 Ere I had learned life's storms to brave,
Grief's gushing floods thy current drank;
 My tears fell mingling with thy wave.

"O, stream that hast my tears," I sighed,
 "And hastenest with them to the sea!
Would that thy depths might sorrow hide,
 That all life's cares were drowned in thee!

But thou would'st scorn to mate with sorrow;
 Peaceful thou journeyest on thy way;
No thought thou takest for the morrow,
 Flowing unruffled day by day.

Would that life's river, smooth as thine,
 Might waft me to some tranquil scene,

Where the sweet light of hope might shine,
  As yon sun in thy floods serene!

While each mute thing forgets its troubles,
  Thought's favored child his watch must keep;
His joys, as transient all as bubbles,
  Sole of all creatures doomed to weep.[37]

Just twenty years, and now at last
  The youth into the man hath ripened;
And memory, smiling o'er the past,
  Hath all the backward landscape brightened.

And now thine ancient guest once more
  Hath come to view thy waters wild;
A child he roamed thy banks of yore,
  And he returns to thee a child;

Still frank, still fond, as in those years
  When first thy flowery marge he ranged,
He brings thee all again but tears;
  Passion is dead, but love unchanged.

Even as thou wast he finds thee still,
  The fields, the flowers as fresh as ever;
The same dark pines tower up yon hill;
  Thou art the same pure, placid river.

Thy smooth and glassy breast gives back
  The image of the same blue sky;
As brownly darkening o'er thy brink
  The rocks o'erhang thee from on high.

O, why no longer in my breast
  Dost thou a pleasing grief excite?
I see thee, but my soul's at rest;
  I view thee with a calm delight.

Have grander scenes made thee seem tame?
  Or hath experience me made dull?
Sweet stream! thou art in all the same;
  I still can deem thee beautiful.

But tears and raptures yield at last
  To weight of more substantial care;
And love, more poor than in the past,
  Foregoes the luxury of despair.

Through Fancy's glass of magic dyes,
  So oft false colors have I seen,
Which changed, when viewed with naked eyes,
  From rosy red to faded green;

So oft I've known fair skies o'ercast,
  And the warm sunshine veiled in showers;

So oft have found a naked waste,
  Where distance clothed the scene with flowers;

So oft, ere youth's first years were past,
  I've laid my loved ones in the dust,
That I have learned, fair stream, at last
  To look on all things with distrust.

Reason hath taught me, without dread,
  My day o'erwhelmed with clouds to see,
And with a careless step to tread
  The bleak wastes of adversity;

To make the most of flower and tree,
  The rather that so soon they fade;
So when a beauteous morn I see,
  She whispers, "It must end in shade."

Therefore I husband it with care,
  Still lengthening pleasure to the last;
And when 'tis o'er I ne'er despair,
  But seek my sunshine in the past,

Or forward, in a fair to-morrow
  The cloudy present I forget,
Nor for one instant harbor sorrow;
  For I have learned, O rivulet!

That absent pain is life's chief pleasure;
 Who 'scapes remorse or dire distress
Hath found on earth no common treasure;
 Few reach so mean a happiness.

In humblest things I find delight,
 Nor seek in man nor thee perfection,
And keep my day, now near its night,
 Warm with a more diffused affection.

And though no brilliant scenes entrance,
 No dull ones cast too deep a shade;
Onward I tranquilly advance,
 Admiring nought, of nought afraid.

I live like one that doubts of joy,
 Ne'er grasp at bliss, but lightly touch;
The man, grown wiser than the boy,
 True pleasure finds in "not too much."

Flow unadmired, then, at my feet;
 Of my old raptures I've repented;
Henceforth, O never seem more sweet
 Than just enough to seem contented.

Yet, though my ecstasies are o'er,
 Love now is from delusion free,

And this calm joy approves thee more
  Than though my tears should fill the sea.

Fair as of old, still freshly flow
  Unchanged, while I, no more the same,
Will hear thy wild voice laugh at woe,
  And charm away all sense of pain.

And now farewell, till coming night
  Upon thy breast shall softly sigh,
And for her brother's dying light
  Weep silent tears of dew, while I,

Who love ye both, will shed no tears.
  Ah, not in rain life's sun must set!
I can but watch with ye. Long years
  Have dried the fountains of regret;
  Taught me to bear, and to forget.

THE OLD AND THE NEW HERO.

'Mid the thick dust of battle I saw thy tall steed
Bear thee onward, brave chieftain! to wound and
to bleed.
Fire and smoke dimmed thy path, and the trum-
pet's loud blast
Sang shrill 'midst the death strokes that round thee
fell fast.
Thy sword gleamed afar, and thy sun-gilded crest
Spilled its feathers, like waterfalls, white o'er thy
breast.
Now soaring, now sinking, now seen, and now
lost,
Still thy voice through the clangor loud called to
thine host.
Rank on rank they press forward; no more I
descry,
For the smoke clouds had swept the bright sun
from the sky.

But when evening crept on, veiled in shadows of
gray,
The smouldering reek drifted slowly away;
And the roar of the battle had melted to moans,
Where the wounded all night vexed the air with
their groans.

No flames from thy musketry glared on the night,
But the fireflies flashed fast, and with innocent light
Mocked their blaze, and the thunders that roared from the hill
Were changed to the chaunt of the lone whip-poorwill,
And while dead men, heaped up, lay in piles far and wide,
The hedge cricket sang her short psalm at their side.

Next year, when I roamed through that sorrowful scene,
Where rivers of blood threaded valleys of green,
The fresh, blooming fields showed no signs of decay;
All traces of slaughter had vanished away.
The rank vines had woven their leaves into bowers,
And the forms of the slain were converted to flowers.
All was tranquil: the wounded had ceased from their groans,
Each slept unmolested, a hillock of bones.
Ten thousand strong men, clad in armor of brass,
All martyred,—for what? to prove flesh is but grass.

But a column of marble towered high on the plain
From the grave of the chief, who his thousands
had slain;
And the hand of the sculptor his story had told,
And called on the pilgrim, to mourn o'er the mould
Of a chief, who died young, but who fought long
and well,
Nor gave o'er, till the last of his enemies fell.
"Farewell," was it writ, "not forgot shalt thou
sleep,
For heroes shall come o'er thy relics to weep;
While bards in sweet songs chaunt the deeds of
the brave,
And glory illumines the gloom of the grave."

"Farewell, then!" said I, "since thy warfare is
ended;
With the dust of these valleys thine also is blended;
Thou mayest thank the dull stone that here guards
thy repose,
That thy fame, like thy carcass, went not to the
crows;
Yet lament, that the sweetness of flattery's breath
For so transient a season, can save thee from death;
For new idols shall fall, to draw tears from the
eyes
Of them that ne'er wept for the good nor the wise.

So the prayer of the ignorant savage ascends
To the God whom he fears, not to him that befriends."

Sons of slaughter! I would that your worship might cease,
That men's hands might be joined in the temples of peace,
And that heroes may herald a new age of gold,
Who shall teach men their swords into ploughshares to mould,
And their spears into pruning hooks; then will be joy
In the brave who save life, not in brutes that destroy.
Ye children of bloodshed, how long must ye slay,
Ere ye sleep undisturbed and forgot, till the day
When the knight and his armor, converted to stones,
Shall be dug up for show, like the mastodon's bones?

Blest shade of the hero, who tranquilly sleeps,
Where the sunny Potomac so joyously sweeps!
Frown not, I intend no irreverence to thee,
Nor to him, thy dear friend, who crossed over the sea,
And left his gay land of the vineyard behind;
Whose sword for defence, and whose heart for mankind,

Leaped both, but at sacred Humanity's call.
Brave foes to oppression! I honor ye all,
Not for bloodshed, ah, no! if I bend to your dust,
'Tis the tribute unconscious I yield to the just.

Yet, Freedom hath friends as devoted, as brave,
Who never drew sword on the field or the wave.
Honored friend of mankind, who so lowly art laid,
Where the cypress of Russia affords thee its shade!
Long wandering a pilgrim through Europe's do-
mains,
To lighten the burden of Infamy's chains!
Though no tears in that wilderness water thy
grave,
Yet thy name shall be dear to the morally brave.
Not for genius men love thee, mild Howard; 'twas
thine
But to teach how the human may reach the divine!

And thou too, O Sharp! whose benevolent mind
Sought in action no end but the good of mankind,
Who the soil of thine England to bondsmen made
free,
Wreathe the fingers of Glory no chaplet for thee,
Since the last of life's tempests hath swept o'er thy
head?
Yes, the halo of virtue shall round thee be shed.

World-citizen, speak! for what conqueror's fame
Wouldst thou yield the mute reverence that clings
to thy name?
Nay, it needs not; thy wish I see stamped on thy
face,
Not to perish for glory, but live for thy race.

Go, citizen soldier! e'en fly to the spade.
I care not how humbly thou dwellest in shade,
So thy thoughts on no schemes of aggrandizement
brood,
No visions of rapine, no phantoms of blood.
O leave the poor Indian his land in the west!
Let the lust of dominion be quenched in thy breast;
Let thy mind in the school of reflection be taught.
To rule action by reason, and passion by thought;
And to deem well repaid all the toils of thy youth,
Hast thou mastered one law in the kingdom of
Truth.

Happy mortal, whose days unembittered with strife,
Have been spent in the peace of an innocent life;
Like the lingering glow of an autumn day's close,
Whose spirit so tranquilly sinks to repose,
That those who so anxiously stand round his bed,
And reverently gaze on the time-honored head,

Can find in death's mildness relief to their fears;
In the smile of content a reproof to their tears;
Nor distinguish, when flies the last fluttering
breath,
The calmness of sleep from the quiet of death.

TO THE MANES OF FIELD MARSHAL HAYNAU;[38]

OF HUNGARIAN MEMORY.

"O, there is joy when hands that held the scourge
Drop lifeless, and the pitiless heart is cold."
BRYANT.—*Hymn to Death.*

ESCAPED from shame at last, yet though deprived
Of earthly reverence, almost, proud knight,
I could have wished thou hadst a while survived,
Nor crossed with Charon in so sore a plight;
Thy stripes paid back, thy chin of beard despoiled,
Thy burly frame with noisome ordure soiled.

Yet why? for though thy livery might, by scrubbing,
Soon have been cleansed; though soap had smoothed thy skin,

And time the scars left by thine English drubbing,
A deeper stain had dyed the man within.
Rest then; there's now no use but one for thee,
To point this maxim of philosophy.

"No man can serve two masters." Thou hadst sold
Life's charities to please thy monarch's will,
And he with gifts requited thee; 'tis well;
But thou to justice wast a bondsman still.
The one rewarded thee with wealth and station;
The other gave thee o'er to condemnation.

Both claimed thy service; but the mightier one
Hath snatched the weaker potentate's reward,
And waiting till thy bloody work was done,
At length disarms thee of thy whip and sword.
Thanks, Justice, that of bad men in disgrace
Canst teachers make, whilst warnings to their race.

Nor yet did Conscience leave thee out of sight;
Not thy new marshal's baton could beguile
The weary soul, which left the world's sweet light
When Fortune had but just begun to smile.
Could not the gifts of thine approving master
Console thee for thy sorrowful disaster?

No, thou hadst lived to learn that Austria's heel
  Trode not the necks of all men, and thy mind,
Howe'er unmerciful, thou couldst not steel
  Against the honest scorn of all mankind.
No, no ; the sword thrusts of a thousand wars
Could ne'er have stung like those disgraceful scars.

What did it boot thee that thou wast so brave
  To slaughter freemen, and to scourge the backs
Of helpless women, since e'en now, poor slave,
  Thy master hath forgotten thee, nor lacks
Thousands of unhanged rogues, that wait his grace
From their unblushing ranks to fill thy place?

Yet do I take no pleasure in thy fall,
  Except for this — that in thy chastisement
I see that the great laws which govern all
  Are not diverted from their wise intent;
I reverence them, not that they punished thee,
But that their force protects humanity.

And though I seem to join the savage rout
  Of brewers, butchers, draymen, and the others,
Who plucked thee by the nose and beard about,
  'Tis not that the law-breakers are my brothers,
Nor that I thirst for blood; but I rejoice
That Freedom dares on earth to lift her voice.

Death strikes in kindness when he smites the hand
  Uplifted 'gainst the poor and the oppressed;
Hunted by all mankind, henceforth what land
  Had sheltered? None; earth had for thee no rest.
Nor can I deem them cruel, I confess,
Who feel small mercy for the merciless.

But why reproach thee? 'Twas no fault of thine
  That tyranny had taught thee to obey,
And cramped thee to the custom of the time;
  The proverb saith, "Each dog must have his day;"
And ere she reach perfection, the young earth
Is doomed to teem with many a monstrous birth.

I wish no worse to despots and their brood
  Than that they perish lastly without pain;
Yet, until Justice' laws be understood,
  And men grown brotherly, such hopes are vain.
The pest of tyrants nations need not rue,
  Whene'er mankind shall to themselves be true.

TIME DISCOVERING TRUTH.

Something I seek I cannot see,
Till cruel fate shall pity me.
In cities vast, in deserts wild,
In vain I'm hunting for my child,
And now, through many thousand years,
Have mourned her loss with fruitless tears.
I've sought her north, south, west, and east,
But since God made the human beast,
The girl is nowhere to be found;
Man hath devoured her, I'll be bound.
Me, too, he would be glad to slay;
Some I hear asking every day,
How dost make out to kill old Time?
But since I've learned the dark design,
I've ground my scythe, till now 'twill reap
An hundred rascals at a sweep;
How sharp and smooth! and bright as gold!
The handle twice as long's the old;
The very shadow of the thing
Might lop two heads off at a fling.
Now if a man should chance to pass,
I'll send him presently to grass;
There's none shall 'scape, whoe'er he be,
Whether a foe to Truth or me.

Yet gladly would I rest from slaughter
If I could only find thee, daughter.
Where art thou, first-born child of mine?
Why dost thou fly thy father Time?

In the silence of the night
Thou art present to my sight;
In each age I hear thee speak,
But when I haste thy form to seek,
The voice is hushed, and thou art fled,
And old dame Prejudice instead
To meet me comes with limping pace,
And mocks me with her loathed embrace.
O'er and o'er deluded, yet
Thee I never can forget.
Where thou art I cannot tell;
But one thing I know full well:
So woven art thou with my heart,
That of myself thou seemest part;
And till my lost one I can find,
I must roam like one that's blind.
O, speak and answer; dost survive?
My daughter, art thou still alive?
Or am I seeking for a sound,
Not for a thing that may be found?
I cannot tell, yet long ago
I should have dropped the search, I know,

Save that 'tis written in the past,
Time shall discover Truth at last.

My throat is dry with calling thee.
Would that some fountain I might see;
Yet now, methinks, I seem to hear
A spring or streamlet bubbling near.
Ah, here's a well; I'll down and drink,
And leave my scythe upon the brink;
Yet first I'll cover it with grass,
Lest it be stol'n by some that pass.
What do I see? that face I know;
Is it my child lies there below,
Still fresh in all her youthful charms?
Come up to thine old father's arms!
What! wilt not speak? Then fate hath lied.
No doubt she hath fallen in and died;
Else to my wrong is joined abuse;
I've found when finding hath no use.
Perhaps she sleeps; for sure, so fair,
No dead thing could lie smiling there.
Awake! alas, beneath, how far!
Her face shines twinkling like a star.
She cannot hear me, and I know
She lies full half a mile below.
Hopeless to reach her, that seems clear;
She's too far down my voice to hear;

Must she for aye lie there forlorn?
She might as well have ne'er been born.
Wake, daughter, wake! and solve my doubt!
How shall thy father fish thee out?

LIFE.

Spirit of life, so lately fled
  From those once sparkling eyes!
That leavest me to mourn the dead
  With useless tears and sighs!

Like a sweet thought thou didst depart,
  Unfelt, unheard, unseen;
Then why laments my foolish heart
  Thus for an empty dream?

Those glassy eyes seem gazing yet,
  Though thou art there no more;
Still smile the lips, which once could "set
  The table in a roar."

Is he not gone, but only mute,
  As when the whispering trees

Hush to a calm, or like a flute
  With none to press the keys?

Ah friend! thine is some deeper death —
  The trees shall sigh once more;
Soon shall the skilled musician's breath
  The flute's sweet sounds restore;

But thou, to silent earth consigned,
  Shalt slumber with the past;
Thy friends shall seek, but shall not find;
  This look must be our last.

And thus, ere long, my loved ones all
  Shall leave me lonely here;
And I must cover with the pall
  All whom my soul holds dear,

With but this thought to soothe the heart,
  In musing on the past, —
That the stern law which bids us part,
  Shall blend our dust at last.

Spirit of life, why yield life's breath?
  Why seek thyself to slay?
Sure, thou art sweeter far than death;
  Bloom lovelier than decay;

Alas, thou wilt not stay thy flight,
  For Wise, or Fair, or Just!
Is day less dear to thee than night,
  Or thought than senseless dust?

LIFE'S ANSWER.

'Tis true, my child, I seem to fly,
  Yet cease thy tears to shed;
Nor falsely deem thy dear ones die,
  Because thou see'st them dead.

Through myriad paths my way I take,
  And as my course I keep,
All things are doomed awhile to wake,
  Awhile to fall asleep.

I thread my way through running streams;
  I laugh in waving trees;
I sport in every sunny beam;
  I murmur in the breeze;

I roam the earth, I ride the storms,
  I swim within the main;
I change to endless varying forms,
  Yet ever am the same.

All shapes of ocean, air, and earth,
  Alternate must decay;
They perish to renew their birth, —
  Thou sayest, "They fade away."

Heed not what form the spirit takes;
  Millions of such there be;
Death seizes upon all my shapes,
  But hath no power o'er me.

Like thee, I do but change a dress
  That's soiled from day to day;
Deem not for this all loveliness
  Is doomed to pass away.

Like thee, I would not always wear
  The torn robes of the past;
And still throw by, with each new year,
  My playthings of the last.

Hath Death's cold finger chilled a heart
  Thou in thine own didst cherish?
Think not thy friend and I shall part;
  Nothing once made can perish.

'Tis only to grow warm once more,
  That he hath now grown cold;

Time seeks his green youth to restore,
  Lest Age might grow too old.

The blast that blights each wasted frame,
  But sets a captive free;
I breathe, and senseless earth again
  Wakes to new liberty.

Deem then no suicide am I,
  Because he sleeps in dust;
Nor falsely think that men must die,
  Because their bodies must.

Go, child of earth, henceforth fear not
  Lest being cease to be;
Till God hath his own self forgot,
  Space shall be filled with me.

And though a race more fair than thou,
  May walk the earth at last,
Wiser and purer, when thy brow
  In rock shall be bound fast,

Deem not for this thy tribes shall cease;
  They shall more perfect be;
Destined in truth and love to increase
  Through all Eternity.

Farewell! to my great Father's side,
The fount of me, I fly.
Rejoice! not that thy friend hath died,
But that he cannot die.

The Almighty Sire who reigns above
Hath me this secret shown;
All life at last shall dwell in love
Eternal, like his own.

A LAST WORD TO "THE WATER-FOWL."

APROPOS TO A WELL KNOWN MASTERPIECE OF AMERICAN POETRY.

Soar on, as when the bard's admiring eyes
Traced thee through twilight glow, and from thy flight
Deduced this just conclusion, that the All-Wise,
Who guided thee, would lead his steps aright.

Fly to thy destined goal, where leaves are green,
And flowers unfading still, though ice and snow,
In thy late haunts, enshrouding all the scene,
Encase each bough, and crust the earth below.

But when once more the new reviving spring
Hath waked each warbler, and each stream unbound,
And cheerful May hath raised her hands to fling
Her flowery carpet o'er the moistened ground,

Again come back, with all thy noisy host,
And with loud cries this constant truth resound:
That nothing through all nature's realm is lost,
That all revolve in one eternal round.

This restless earth, each planetary sphere,
The breath of life, winds, tides, the cloud, the rill,
Go and return like thee, all taught to steer
Through fixed cycles, by the Eternal will.

ODE TO TRUTH

FIRST TREATMENT.

TRUTH PERSUASIVE.

O THOU, that in thyself content,
Wilt not be moved by argument!
That growest more fair with growing old!
Deemed by the fool, severe and cold,

But by the wise, more precious far
Than all things that most beauteous are!
Dwelling unveiled in heavenly light,
Thou wilt be served but by the upright;
And none thy lustre can endure
Save the unspotted soul and pure.
How blest are they that join thy train,
Far from the proud, the false, the vain,
Within thy sacred haunts, serene that dwell,
And at the crystal waters of thy well,
Quench knowledge' thirst, and hear thy tongue relate
How Love paternal did all things create;
All dear alike to him that governs all,[39]
The starry world so vast, the earth so small,
Down to the humblest moss that grows upon the wall!

O Maid divine! sometimes in mists of doubt
So densely veiled, that few can find thee out;
Yet to the steadfast seeker ever kind,
Permitting the most patient, first to find;
To the long tried thou lov'st to show
Wisdom that worldlings cannot know,
And wilt with eloquent lips explain
The natural laws, in wondrous chain,

Each to each linkéd without end;
God wilt thou show, of His own works the friend,
Bending to order each, with just direction,
And each sustaining, with a wise affection,
That all for aye improve, yet never reach perfection.

Instructress wise! fain would I stand
As one among thy chosen band,
Forgetting fear, and care, and folly;
But, wrapped in pleasing melancholy,
Hang on thy lips, and feel the day
Pass in unanxious peace away!
And when the moon sets sail on high,
And stars are lit through all the sky,
From each far lighthouse, twinkling through
Those boundless seas of limpid blue,
Still would I muse in calm so deep
That thought itself should seem like sleep;
While days, and months, and years glide by
In studious calm, so noiselessly,
That lastly, scarce the dart of death
Should startle, when it stopped my breath.
O Truth, what pleasures so divine can be,
As feels the soul that tranquil dwells with thee,
At peace with man, and with itself in harmony!

ODE TO TRUTH.

SECOND TREATMENT.

TRUTH CONTEMPLATIVE.

O Truth, from Error's barren waste
A pilgrim comes thy fount to taste;
One, on whose youth thy countenance smiled;
Though from thy paths too long beguiled,
The way to thee is half forgot,
Till haply thou wilt know him not,
But veil thee in so black a cloud,
As shall thy sacred haunts enshroud,
And hide the thousand ways that lead,
Each by a slight and brittle thread,
To that fair fane, where, robed in white,
And crowned with rays of clearest light,
Thou, from the vulgar gaze concealed,
Art only to pure eyes revealed.

O, child of Heaven! in days of old,
I deemed thee stern, thy fountain cold;
Yet Error from thy paths away
Entices e'en thy friends to stray,
Charmed by Delusion's magic light,
Gleaming from fens, yet briefly bright,
Which tempts to death, and ends in night.

Truant awhile, to thy domain
The wanderer hath returned again;
For time can ne'er thy charms efface
From eyes that once have known thy face;
And though thou surely wilt not deign
To rank me of thy household train,
And though thy stair I may not mount,
To fill my pitcher at thy fount,
Yet sometimes at thine outer gate,
With Science' servants do I wait,
Discoursing of thy worth, while she
Sits in thine inner courts with thee;
And oft, some wandering muse to meet,
Ere the first warblers wake, my feet
Over the lawns and meadows pass,
Brushing the dew drops from the grass;
And when night is drawing near,
And the fenny choirs I hear
From the meadows piping clear,
Mingled with the cowbell's clink,
Where the herds have stopped to drink,
While brooding silence casts her spell
O'er dewy dale, and dreamy dell;
Then, oft, with meditation met,
All things of earth do I forget,
Through bushy by-paths wandering far
By the light of evening star,

Till distant chimes with drowsy hum
Proclaim the hour of rest is come,
And warn me with the dying bell
Once more to seek the studious cell,
Where Morpheus seldom comes to knock
Till early dawn hath waked the cock;
From night till morn, from morn till night,
Thy worship an unmixed delight.

Thus would I serve thee day by day,
Till old age shall make me gray;
And though 'twere vain to hope mine eyes
Should e'er make out the sense that lies
In thy more secret mysteries,
Yet wilt thou deem he serves thee well,
Who some few words can faintly spell,
If it so be with cheerful will,
And humble heart, he seeks thee still.
To him, ofttimes, the winged hours
Will waft some music from thy bowers,
Or, from thy language heard in part,
Imprint a lesson on his heart.

O, guide divine! how blest is he,
Who early learns to walk with thee.
His house Despair ne'er enters in;
Grim Death no terrors hath for him;

His life glides on like some fair river,
Deeper, broader, calmer ever;
Still fertilizing as it flows,
While winds scarce ruffle its repose.
Him no disasters can appall;
He feareth not what may befall;
The heavens and earth to him are musical.
And if the senses e'er have power
To bind thy votary for an hour,
Folly can never hold him long,
Who the mean joys of feast and song
Hath measured with those rare delights
Wherewith Philosophy invites;
Friends, books, and thought, and all those joys
Which most disdain the haunts of noise;
The rustic cot with gardens neat,
Far from the city's crowded street,
There, when the day's dull toils are ended,
To be with contemplation friended,
Lifted above all thought of sorrow,
Or of the strife that comes to-morrow;
And, when summer heats are nigh,
To some lonelier haunt to fly;
The pensive grove, the solemn wood,
The green hills breezy solitude,
Or smooth worn beaches, where the sea
Sighs with a soft monotony,

Or lodge forlorn in sleepy dale,
Muffled in mountain shadows pale,
Where, through the cool sequestered glade,
E'en noon comes swathed in twilight shade.
All these full oft in bygone age
Were dear to wandering saint and sage,
Seeking some wild, secluded place,
To question Nature face to face.

Yet if the sons of strife, even here,
With din of discord draw too near,
Then let forest depths invite,
Where songs of birds and brooks delight,
While the cataract in the breeze
Blends with the roaring of the trees;
Or, where the wild deer roams the glen,
Unstartled at the steps of men,
While Echo sleeps her cliffs among,
Ne'er waked by noise of axe or tongue.
Here, sheltered in some snug retreat
From winter's snows and summer's heat,
O Truth! I'd dwell with Peace and thee,
Wrapped in a blest obscurity.
Here oft thy footsteps would I trace,
Musing along with solemn pace;
Here sometimes meet thee face to face;

While life, in thoughtful leisure spent,
Longs not to soar beyond content,
The highest bliss of Fate we borrow
That is not mingled with some sorrow.

ODE TO CELESTIAL LOVE.

TAMER of hearts, whose life began
Long ere the transient race of man
Roamed o'er the yet uncultured earth!
Thine eyes beheld creation's birth,
And saw the heaving ocean shroud
The giant hills in billowy cloud;
While o'er the vast unbroken deep
Silence in darkness lay asleep.
Ere yet the animating breath
Swept o'er the wastes of watery death,
Thou, sleepless, in the Eternal Mind,
Watched through those ages long and blind,
In thine unbounded glance foreseeing
The chain of uncreated being.

Time didst thou rock, while yet he slept;
Till the young infant tottering crept;

Then didst thou watch, lest he might fall—
The hoary father of us all!
Nursed him, that he might grow, and bless
Earth with unending fruitfulness.

Through thee the Almighty Father wrought,
While yet He brooded, wrapped in thought,
With countenance veiled, musing the fate
Of what ere long He might create;
Then, first-born of immortal race,
He smiled benignant on thy face;
"In thee," He said, "my likeness will I cherish;
Fear not, my daughter, lest thou e'er should'st
perish;
Though Time, thy son, must die when he grows old,
And all his children mingle with the mould,
Thou shalt not fail. Go, child of my affection:
Go; join thy gentleness to my reflection,
And bring our world at last to its perfection.
Do thou add joy, while I inspire with thought,
Till matter all with soul be interwrought."
Then gave he for thy symbol his own dove,
And, thy blest immortality to prove,
He called thee from himself, and said: "Thy name
be Love."

NOTES.

NOTES.

1. "*Nathan Hale.*" For the most authentic account of him, see "The Life of Benedict Arnold," by Jared Sparks.

2. "*Samuel Adams.*" Few materials exist for preserving his memoirs; partly, because being of an unselfish disposition, he preferred the independence of his country to the reputation of being a principal achiever of it; and partly, because after the death of his wife, most of his papers were abstracted, and only partially recovered by the persistent industry of his grandson, the late S. A. Wells, who profoundly venerated him, and in resolution of character resembled him.

The death of Mr. Wells in 1841, when the first volume of his "Life of Samuel Adams" was nearly through the press, prevented the completion of that work.

In the present poem the author has wished to preserve among others a few interesting memorials of this eminent patriot, which might otherwise perish with the oral traditions that have thus far preserved them in his family.

3. "*Arguing that much vexed question,*" &c. "Is it lawful to resist the supreme magistrate, if the commonwealth cannot be otherwise preserved?" The subject of his thesis on receiving the degree of A. M., 1743; he maintained the affirmative.

4. "*How trifling in thine eyes seemed worldly wealth,*" &c. Neglecting his private affairs for those of his country, and unwilling to press the payment of debts due from others, he much reduced a considerable property left him by his father. Superior to all mercenary motives, and careless of personal safety where duty was concerned, he long performed the most arduous public services, almost without compensation.

5. "*Or that with bribes they tempted thee,*" &c. The fact is generally known. Mr. Wells related to the author, that he had been informed that the late secretary of state, Mr. Avery, possessed papers, which contained offers to Mr. Adams of a patent of nobility and ten thousand pounds per annum, provided he would cease from opposing the government; but Mr. Avery had been long dead, and the biographer had in vain sought a clew to the discovery of these papers.

6. "*My peace has long been made,*" &c. His answer to Colonel Fenton, when sent to silence him by means of bribes and threats. He added, "Tell Governor Gage it is the advice of Samuel Adams to him, no longer to insult the feelings of an exasperated people."

7. "*I wait thine answer*," &c. Interview with Governor Hutchinson and council, when, after the Boston massacre, the people demanded the removal of the regiments. "I observed his knees to tremble, I saw his face grow pale, and I enjoyed the sight." Letter to Warren. See Bancroft's "Hist. U. S.," vol. vi. chap. 43.

8. "*Thou soughtest in one will*," &c. Samuel Adams was the originator of the plan for appointing committees of correspondence throughout the states, and from him R. H. Lee and James Warren derived their ideas on this subject.

Teste, S. A. Wells.

9. Morning of the 19th April, 1775.

10. "*If of a thousand, all*," &c. Several versions of this remark are recorded. He was the friend of universal liberty, and in different instances, becoming the master of female slaves by the death of relatives, he made them free, and allowed them the wages of white servants.

11. "*Because thou gav'st to flame*," &c. He was unwilling to retain what might compromise others.

12. "*Feast on her cast up clams*," &c. From a speech made during the excitement which followed the tea act.

Teste, S. A. Wells.

13. " *Thou didst add, be't understood,*" &c. The same expression also occurred in a letter to his daughter, which letter was afterwards lost.

14. " *When men once strove to unloose,*" &c. This incident occurred during a public procession, and was at various times related by his daughter, in the presence of her children.

15. " *Guilt only feared thy frown.*" He was of a benignant aspect, of gracious manners, and was indulgent toward innocent foibles, being wont to remark that vice only is contemptible. He detested all cruelty, and among other instances of his humanity, his daughter was accustomed to relate that an urgent letter from him saved on one occasion a British soldier from five hundred lashes.

16. "*No idle statue apes thine air.*" The principal memorials of the person of Samuel Adams are as follows: First, the picture by Copley, which represents him in the attitude of an orator. It was painted for Governor Hancock, became afterwards the property of Mr. Wells, and is now in Faneuil Hall. A spirited engraving was made from it, by T. House, for the work of Mr. Wells; but only a few proofs have been taken from the plate. Second, a full length, taken in old age, by Johnston. He is seated in an arm-chair, his hand resting on a chart, and an open window discloses a view of the old State House in Boston. It was faithfully engraved in mezzotinto, by Graham, in

1797, and the print, which is in folio, is of the extremest scarcity.

17. "*And o'er the uncolumned tomb,*" &c. Samuel Adams was buried in the Checkley tomb, which adjoins the westerly sidewalk of Tremont street, in Boston. His bones have been gathered into a box by his grandson, and deposited in a corner of the vault.

Teste, S. A. WELLS.

ASSABET BROOK AND RIVER.

18. The Assabet river rises in Worcester county, Mass., is joined in Stowe by the Assabet brook, and uniting in Concord with the Sudbury, forms the Concord river proper, which empties into the Merrimack at Lowell.

19. "*Since now the artist's skilful hand,*" &c. Some interesting drawings made by Mr. Henry Hitchings, the landscape draughtsman, are here referred to.

20. "*Where near the verge the Ball flowers blow;*" i. e. "*Cephalanthus occidentalis,*" *Linn.* Commonly called "button bush."

21. "*Near that gray column rude and low;*" i. e. the battle monument in Concord.

THE SOLITARY MAN.

22. "*They seek the false, who have not found the true.*" For an amplification of which idea, see Montaigne's Fourth Essay.

THE MOUNTAIN JOURNEY.

23. The laws which regulate the geographical distribution of plants, in accordance with which altitude becomes the representative of latitude, have been well known to naturalists since the days of De Saussure. The same phenomena which are observable upon European mountains, occur also with slight variations upon our own. A few facts may here suffice for the unscientific reader.

After having penetrated, upon one of our loftier New England ranges, the forests of oak, maple, &c., we find ourselves in the region of birches, which, more or less intermingled with pines, continue to surround us, until we have reached a great height; their trunks frequently of a large size, yet growing in so loose a soil, that when grasped by the hands, they may sometimes be made to swing from side to side with the greatest ease. Meantime the dense, spongy carpet of moss heaves beneath our feet, and if we examine this moss, especially in steep situations, we shall find that the roots of the trees ramify its substance, often for long distances; and if we look more closely, we shall see that it conceals numberless little cisterns of water, formed in the hollows of the rocks, from which moisture is abundantly supplied for the nourishment both of the mosses and of the trees which they sustain. In our latitude, at a height of less than five thousand feet, we find ourselves at the limit of forest trees, and, near this limit, we frequently arrive at a dense, narrow belt of dwarf firs, only a few feet in height, which seem as if formed in regimental line; their branches declining, and so rigid, that it is nearly impossible to penetrate their ranks; for while the depending limbs readily permit one to slip down between the trunks, to extricate oneself is not so easy, as the tattered clothing of the traveller frequently testifies. Above this point, we find only stunted bushes, intermingled with slender trunks, blasted and bleached, the skeletons of a race long since perished, and here we frequently reach a terrace, enough depressed to hold here and there little lakes, on whose margins grow various rare plants, mostly unknown in the regions below. Soon we arrive at a pyramid composed of broken rocks, piled one upon another, and this forms the peak, which first strikes the eye from a distance, when in looking toward one of our granite ranges one descries a series of broad, rounded bases, for the most part surmounted by cones more or less sharpened. As we scramble with difficulty over this rude pile of rocks, all verdure disappears; we are surrounded only by desolation. At last the top is reached, and suddenly in this region of mists the foot treads upon dense carpets formed by the snow-white blossoms of different species of Arenarias, whose flowers are much larger than those of the insignificant kinds which grow upon the plains. Very interesting is it to observe these changes in vegetation. The higher one climbs, the more arctic will be the character of the flora, especially as regards genera; and in the journey of a morning, the traveller, were he to judge of the distance he has measured by the plants which he meets with, will seem to have traversed several degrees of latitude.

24. "*No poisonous shrub of sickly hue.*" Poisonous plants do not inhabit the higher mountain regions; in Alpine flowers moreover the colors are more often simple than mixed — the white and the rosaceous seem to predominate over the blue and the yellow; they are for the most part scentless, because fragrance, to reach its highest perfection, requires a warm and dry climate. Stems of woody fibre yield also to the succulent, the rough and spinous to the smooth, the long to the short, annual plants to perennial ones, and all perhaps for similar reasons, viz.: their dependence for nutrition rather upon moisture than the soil, and the brief time allotted to their development. Not only are the Alpine species larger flowered than their congeners in the lowlands, but even species, which are common to a great range of latitude, hurried to perfection by a short summer and the constant trickling of melted snows, flourish in mountain districts with the most vigor and in greatest abundance. Nowhere will one find the Azaleas more splendid than on the summit of the Wachusett mountain. Still farther north, other species occur. In the elevated regions about the Moosehead lake, the swamps are filled with the Rhodora Canadensis in extraordinary perfection. The very islands of the lake are red with it. Different species of Trillium, Corydalis, Epilobium, &c., with various orchideous plants, ornament the mountain bases, while the "Dracæna borealis," which accompanies us for long distances up their sides, enlivens the greater portion of the year, at an earlier season, with its flowers of a golden yellow, and at

a later, with its berries of a celestial blue. The true Rhododendrons, which so greatly adorn the European mountains, and those of our middle states, are perhaps less frequent; but their place is supplied in the far north by the beautiful Kalmia glauca, one of the finest species of its genus, while on the very summits of the highest peaks, especially upon the Grand Haystack in New Hampshire, the bold and savage Mt. Bigelow in Maine, and the White Mountains proper, the above-mentioned Arenarias, and more rarely, the Lapland Diapensia, whose brief awakening is succeeded by a long sleep of many months, enliven the very loftiest summits, blossoming among the banks of snow which lie piled around them, and creating a garden in the clouds, nay, sometimes too much elevated above them to receive nourishment from the raindrops which they scatter.

25. "*But passed the pine and birchen grove.*" In the mountains of the north of Europe, the birch has the highest range, but as far as the observation of the author has extended, the pines reach a higher altitude in New England, which is rich in the cone-bearing trees.

26. "*All new! the very insect race.*" The limits of the animal are as rigidly defined as those of the vegetable kingdom. Seas and mountain barriers divide races from each other; and this law of parallelism, between altitude and latitude, seems to include even the insect world. In the highlands of Maine and New Hampshire, occurs a

Canadian Fauna, and various new species of insects, which did not occur in the lowlands, were there formerly observed by the author, some of which were, nearly at the same time, collected by Dr. Richardson's exploring party, in the extreme north of the British possessions; a circumstance favorable to the theory which deduces the origin of animal and vegetable forms from many centres, rather than one.

27. "*And as the clouds beneath thy feet.*" The great variety of atmospheric effects presents some of the most interesting traits in mountain scenery, as when in a foggy morning the white veil slowly rising displays all the lower landscape clearly to the eye; while on the greater peaks wreaths piled upon wreaths are broken into a thousand picturesque shapes, and soar so high in air that the observer is deceived as to the real height of the ridges before him; which in districts of even moderate elevation, seem like vast Alpine ranges covered with eternal snow. As he ascends, he finally enters this region of vapors, which as they grow thinner and thinner, become at last so penetrated by the diffused sunlight, that every particle is illuminated; and if he look behind him, the earth so suddenly terminates in a sea of mist, that the steep pyramid up which he is clambering appears like a precipitous island floating in a magic sky, amidst a drizzly rain of infinitesimal diamonds.

Not less beautiful are the approach and retreat of storm-clouds, when thunders, at first heard in the distance, sound nearer, till at last the noise becomes deafening, and the lightnings seem to take aim at our very eyes. Presently the fogs grow thinner; a sunbeam bursts through; the vapory masses begin to scatter; suddenly a cloud rolls toward us; it envelops us; and for a while all is dark again.

Gradually, light prevails; the floating masses separate more and more, sinking lower and lower as they evaporate; and now, far down, an ocean of clouds appears like a new sky. Soon, through some rent, the lower world is disclosed; a distant spire appears; rivers, valleys, forests and villages come in sight; and now the detached islands of mist, striking the lower peaks, become more and more subdivided; and while each pale cloud floats like a ship, with majestic slowness through the airy sea, its sable shadow is seen far below, darkening the earth where it falls, till the eye, fixed involuntarily upon the fantastic and ever varying forms of these vapory ghosts, which, some soaring over head and some swimming beneath our feet, on all sides surround us, becomes bewildered with the endless metamorphoses of light and shade.

ODE TO OBLIVION.

28. "*But science' eye,*" &c., refers to the artificial processes employed for unrolling and deciphering these ancient manuscripts.

SPRING MORNING OF A BEREAVED MAN.

29. "*Then the brown butterfly,*" &c. Vanessa Antiope.

Linn. Apparently the same as the European species, and one of the earliest of its tribe.

MAUSOLEUM OF BURNS.

30. "*Did those sweet lines with truth agree,*" &c.

> "But yet the light that led astray
> Was light from heaven."
> "*The Vision,*" *Duan Second.*

POET AND TOLL-GATHERER.

31. That the toll-man should make a pun involving words of different languages seems to be a natural result of his miscellaneous intercourse with poets of all nations.

32. "*Ofttimes a dozen halt or maimed.*" Probably members of societies instituted for the purpose of mutual admiration.

33. "*Till lost Pompeii's wrecks revealed.*" Because amongst these the trombone was in modern times discovered.

34. "*That class which Plato hath derided.*" See "The Republic" of Plato, but more particularly the image of the Heraclean stone or Magnet, in the "Ion."

VISION OF THE WESTERN WORLD.

35. "*Who life to that pale marble gave,*" &c. This beautiful statue, viz.: the Belvidere Tiber, is the same which has been so finely engraved by Laugier.

MEDICEAN VENUS.

36. "*Where he had been so niggardly of brains.*" The forehead in this statue is small.

THE REVISITED RIVER.

37. "*Sole of all creatures doomed to weep.*" Some other animals are, however, said to weep.

38. "*Marshal Haynau.*" The cruelties of this officer during the late Hungarian revolution, his expulsion from a brewery in London, his castigation by a mob, his concealment in a privy, his flight from England, his contemptuous reception upon the continent, his appointment to the rank of field marshal, by way of consolation, and his death, which quickly followed, are all circumstances too recent and too well known to need explanation here.

39. The word Love, herein several times personified, (not in the sense of Amor,) has been made masculine or feminine as the case required. Here Divine Love is meant, referred to by a pronoun in the masculine. In most other instances, it has been used in the sense of Benevolence, or the Latin *Caritas*, and then made feminine, as in "The Soul's Invocation," q. v. "She our physician," &c.

www.ingramcontent.com/pod-product-compliance
Lightning Source LLC
LaVergne TN
LVHW010240110826
845151LV00004B/1349
9781425523602